CONSISTENCY
AND
COGNITION

A Theory of Causal Attribution

CONSISTENCY
AND
COGNITION

A Theory of Causal Attribution

Shelley Duval
Virginia Hensley Duval

In collaboration with F. Stephan Mayer
University of Southern California

LEA LAWRENCE ERLBAUM ASSOCIATES, PUBLISHERS
1983   Hillsdale, New Jersey   London

Lawrence Erlbaum Associates, Inc. Publishers
365 Broadway
Hillsdale, New Jersey 07642

Library of Congress Cataloging in Publication Data

Duval, Shelley.
  Consistency and cognition.

  Bibliography: p.
  Includes index.
  1. Cognition.   2. Causation.   3. Attribution (Social
psychology)   I. Duval, Virginia Hensley.   II. Mayer,
F. Stephan.   III. Title. [DNLM: 1. Cognition.
2. Psychological theory. BF 311 D983c]
BF311.D886   1983   153   82-21079
ISBN 0-89859-220-8

Printed in the United States of America
10 9 8 7 6 5 4 3 2 1

Contents

Preface

As Jones and Kelley (1978) point out, theories of causal attribution fall into one of two distinct categories: Those that are concerned with the basic psychological processes underlying causal attribution and those that deal with the motivational, affective, and behavioral consequences of causal assignation. Our theory falls into the first category and is based on one major assumption. Causal attribution is a manifestation of the tendency for consciousness, as a system, to organize cognitive content, that is, cognitions, into the simplest structures possible. The following issues are addressed from this theoretical perspective. (1) Why dos causal attribution happen at all? (2) How does the structure of cognitive organization change when causality for an effect is first attributed to an event, and how can this new structure best be described? (3) What principles determine which event will be connected with an effect in a cause-effect relationship? (4) What properties of effects and possible causes constitute independent variables in the attribution process? (5) To what extent do internal systems contribute to those properties?

Our theory is based on certain assumptions about the nature and operation of human consciousness. Consequently, we have drawn freely from works that, in our opinion, have made critical contributions to this area of inquiry. In particular, the theory incorporates certain concepts and language from four sources: Heider's (1944, 1958) application of general principles of cognitive organization to causal attribution, the general principles embodied in cognitive consistency theories of cognitive activity, Tversky's (1977) analysis of asymmetrical relations, and theories of attention.

The present monograph should be interesting to those who find the major questions concerning the attribution process itself interesting. We also believe that the psychologist involved in applying an attributional approach to social interaction, aggression, attitude formation, etc., will find the work thought provoking and, hopefully, useful. Accurate predictions concerning the impact of causal attribution on behavior obviously require ideas concerning what variables influence the attribution process. In this regard, the present work presents several new variables (affective intensity, coping ability) for consideration and invites the reader to look at some of the variables already in use (temporal covariation, violation of expectation) from a new perspective.

At this point we would like to take the opportunity to thank the many people who have contributed to this book. In particular we would like to thank Bob Arkin and Ken Siegel for their helpful comments on earlier versions of the book. Joanne Ramirez has done a remarkable job of typing the numerous drafts that this manuscript has gone through. Our special thanks go to Tony and Julie Lamb.

S.D.
V.H.D.

Introduction

For over 35 years, social psychologists have recognized the importance of causal attribution in determining behavior. Heider's (1944, 1958) suggestion—that a person's ability to control his or her environment depends on the recognition of causal relationships—constitutes the initial statement of the relationship between attribution and behavior. To negotiate the external world, it is certainly advantageous, and possibly essential, to understand which specific events are causing what particular effects. The role of this process in determining behavior is clarified by Kelley's (1973) statement that: "causal attribution identifies the causes of certain effects and forms the basis for decisions about how to act in order to bring about the continuance or discontinuance of those effects [p. 127]." That a person's behavior in a particular situation may be affected by what that person sees as causing a particular effect highlights the need for a theory providing an integrated approach to the dynamics of the causal-attribution process.

TOWARD AN INTEGRATED THEORY
OF CAUSAL ATTRIBUTION

Goal-directed models and models with no implied goal state constitute the two major approaches to the study of cognitive psychology, which, by implication, includes the phenomenon of causal attribution. Goal-directed models assume that consciousness is a homeostatic or teleological system. This type of system has several critical characteristics (Rudner, 1966). First, it attempts to maintain one particular state (or class of states) out of all the possible states it could assume. This state is typically referred to as the *preferred* or *goal state* of the system. Second, if the preferred state is disrupted, the system will exhibit a tendency to reestablish that state. Cognitive dissonance theory (Festinger, 1957) is an example of a goal-directed model of cognition. The preferred state is defined as consonance between and among cognitions. If this state is disrupted through the introduction of dissonant cognitions, the system acts to reestablish consonance by changing cognitions, by adding cognitions, etc. All cognitive consistency theories as well as theories that posit a tendency to enhance or protect self-esteem and perceived control are based on similar assumptions, although the preferred state is defined differently in each case. Thus, even though the goal-directed approach has not yet been fully applied to causal attribution, any such model would argue that causal-attribution processes and the outcomes of such processes reflect the tendency for consciousness to reestablish the preferred state of the system.

In contrast, nongoal-directed models assume that cognitive processes and their outcomes are not governed by any tendency to move toward a preferred state. Instead, they are determined by: (1) properties of cognitive architecture (e.g., attention, memory, categories); (2) a set of rules that specifies what information is relevant to a particular decision; (3) a set of rules that determines how relevant information will be combined to yield that decision. This approach has been applied to causal attribution; in fact, it constitutes the basis for most extant theories. For example, Taylor and Fiske (1978) propose that causal attribution is a function of properties of attention, memory, and a rule specifying that causality for some effect will be attributed to the possible cause that is most readily retrieved from memory. Kelley (1967) suggests that patterns of covariation between effects and possible causes, analyzed within an analysis of variance framework, provide an adequate basis for a theory of causal attribution. According to this view, sequences in which events occur are first simply recorded. A record of an actual cause–effect relationship is assumed to exist if a sequence consists of an event B always occurring after another event A and never occurring unless A precedes it (i.e., A and B covary). Given multiple observations, a naive analysis of variance of covariation matrices determines causality. In the absence of multiple observations, a person determines causality by applying learned schemata (e.g., discounting, augmentation, etc.) to data sequences (Kelly, 1973). Deviation from the patterns of attribution predicted by this model has generally been assumed to result from distortions of the data to which the principle of covariation, naive analysis of variance, and the various schemata are applied (Ross, 1977).

We prefer the goal-directed approach for several reasons. First, none of the nongoal-directed models appear capable of offering a fully integrated theory of causal attribution. Each model deals with a particular set of variables, and there is very little overlap between them. For example, Kelley's model does a reasonable job in dealing with the variables of consensus, distinctiveness, and consistency over time, but it seems unable to cope with the influence of salience on causal attribution. Similarly, Taylor and Fiske's model can deal with salience but not consensus, distinctiveness, or consistency over time. A model of causal attribution based on the goal-directed approach may offer a solution to this lack of theoretical integration. Second, in our opinion, one of the major reasons for the decline of goal-directed theories lies in their assumption that the preferred state is reestablished through distortion of cognition and/or cognitive processes. This is an unnecessary assumption that is probably incorrect. Movement toward a preferred state can be accomplished through processes of organization rather than through distortion just as a jigsaw puzzle can be solved by the appropriate placement of pieces rather than by reshaping the parts. Finally, and perhaps most important, the goal-directed approach simply seems more viable in general than the nongoal-directed orientation. For instance, evidence clearly indicates that biological organization is homeostatic in nature and that behavior is goal-directed. Given this fact, it would be truly surprising if consciousness were not a homeostatic system and if causal attribution were not a goal-directed process. The necessity of including a general goal state as a component of computer simulated models of human problem-solving processes reinforces this conclusion.

Thus, the purpose of this book is to present a goal-directed approach to causal attribution. Our approach is based on the following assumptions:

1. Causal attribution represents the outcome of the tendency for consciousness to reestablish a preferred state. This state is defined as maximum simplicity of cognitive organization.

2. An effect event introduced into consciousness will be joined with a possible cause such that simplicity of cognitive organization is maximized.

3. Movement toward the preferred state is accomplished through the processes of organization rather than through distortion either in the content of cognition or in the processes of cognitive organization.

4. The materials on which the system operates are the internal representations of events (i.e., events as they are cognized). The properties of these cognized events are a product of properties of the external events themselves and the properties of cognitive systems that translate or participate in the translation of the external into the internal.

This theoretical approach is further developed in the following chapter.

CONSISTENCY
AND
COGNITION

A Theory of Causal Attribution

1

Concepts and Theory

Heider (1944, 1958) as well as other psychologists propose that consciousness prefers simplicity. This preference implies that consciousness is a dynamic process that moves to maximize simplicity within its boundaries. Simplicity is an inverse function of the number of separate and unconnected elements in consciousness (i.e., diversity). Maximum simplicity represents the case in which all elements are connected (i.e., minimal diversity). We submit that causal attribution is a manifestation of this movement to maximize simplicity within consciousness. Specifically, awareness of a discrete event that is not spontaneously assimilated to any preexisting cognitive structure decreases simplicity of cognitive organization by increasing the number of separate and unconnected elements in consciousness. The movement toward maximizing simplicity in terms of minimizing diversity connects the event with other elements present in consciousness. The formation of these higher order cognitive structures, which Heider refers to as *unit formations*, reduces diversity because the previously separate element (i.e., the event) is now connected to another or other elements. If one element of a unit formation is defined as an "effect" event and is connected with another event such that they become temporally ordered aspects of a single extended cause-effect sequence, then the unit-formation process is a process of causal attribution. The fact that the elements of a cause–effect unit formation are connected and thus reflect the movement to maximize simplicity is clearly demonstrated by Michotte's (1963) research on the phenomenological characteristics of perceived physical causality. If the movement of an object (B, the effect event) is perceived as caused by contact with another moving object (A), then B's movement is seen as a continuation of the movement of A rather than as a discrete and separate event. The fact that observing or thinking of the occurrence of one element in the cause–effect unit (e.g., a person observes someone turning on the ignition switch of a car) tends to call to mind the other event included in that formation (the person expects the car's engine to start) is further evidence that previously separate cognitions (i.e., turning on the switch, the starting of the engine) are now elements of a single, although extended, cognitive structure.

The movement toward maximum simplicity in terms of minimizing diversity explains why cause–effect units are formed. The attribution process connects events in cause–effect unit formations in order to reduce the number of separate, unconnected elements in consciousness and thus reduce the diversity within that system. However, we must point out that this process is not indiscriminate. A particular effect is not simply connected with all other events in consciousness nor does each event in consciousness have an equal probability of being connected with the effect in a cause–effect unit. These facts suggest that simplicity of consciousness is not solely a function of diversity in the system. A discussion of this issue follows.

In general, it seems reasonable to assume that unit formations made up of elements that are consistent with each other are simpler than unit formations made up of inconsistent elements. This assumption implies that simplicity of consciousness is a function of the degree of consistency between the elements of unit formations as well as the extent to which elements in consciousness are connected together. Specifically, to maximize simplicity the elements in consciousness would not only have to be connected, but connected in units made up of elements that are maximally consistent with each other. *Maximally consistent* is defined as the case in which the elements of unit formations are more consistent with each other than with any other elements in consciousness.

It now appears that simplicity within consciousness is a function of two factors: diversity and consistency. Inasmuch as we have argued that causal attribution is a manifestation of the tendency to maximize simplicity, the dynamics of the causal-attribution process should reflect the operation of these two factors. Movement toward maximum simplicity in terms of minimizing diversity predicts the general tendency to connect effects and other events in cause–effect unit formations; movement toward maximum simplicity in terms of maximal consistency predicts which particular events will be linked with specific effects in cause–effect units. To achieve maximum consistency in cause–effect unit formations, the attribution process tends to join a particular effect with the event that is more consistent with it than are other events present in consciousness. If the person becomes aware of an event that is even more consistent with the effect than the event previously linked with that effect, the tendency to generate maximally consistent cause–effect unit formations will reorganize cognition so that the more consistent event becomes linked with the effect in a new cause–effect unit.

We have proposed that causal attribution represents the constructive processes of cognitive organization. Within consciousness, the movement toward maximum simplicity leads to the organization of effects and other events into higher order cause–effect unit formations whose elements (i.e., the cause and the effect) are maximally consistent with each other. The following example illustrates the hypothesized operation of this dynamic process.

An instructor finds that the class average on a midterm exam is unusually high. On the same day he receives a phone call from a lawyer informing him that his wife is filing for divorce. In neither case is the cause for these events readily apparent (i.e., the instructor does not immediately know why the exam scores were higher than usual nor why his wife is filing for divorce). Now let us assume that the set of events present in the instructor's consciousness is limited to the following: (1) he has recently suffered substantial financial losses; (2) that semester, he changed the format of the lectures presented to his class; (3) his car would not start that morning; (4) he had an argument with his wife concerning the condition of their lawn; (5) the air conditioning was working in the classroom for the first time in several days when the midterm exam was given; (6) his neighbor had a baby on the morning of the midterm. Later, we find that the instructor has attributed causality for the high test scores to the change in the format of his lectures, although he remains somewhat bothered by the fact that he did not actually change the format very much. We also discover that he has attributed causality for his wife's actions to his recent financial setbacks, but he recalls that, even though she was upset, his wife seemed to cope with the financial problems fairly well. On the following day, his teaching assistant informs him that the tests were scored incorrectly. He reattributes causality for the unusually high scores to the error in grading. He also speaks to his wife that day, and she informs him that she is desperately in love with another man. He reattributes his wife's request for a divorce to her relationship with the other man.

The example presents a sequence of events typical of the attribution process. The person first becomes aware of an effect (or effects) for which the cause is not known and then attributes causality for that effect to some other event. If an event that seems to be a better causal explanation is discovered, reattribution occurs. From the present point of view, the events associated with this process reflect the tendency for consciousness to maximize simplicity within its boundaries. First, awareness of two effects (the high test scores and his wife's actions) that were not spontaneously assimilated to preexisting structures decreased simplicity within consciousness by increasing the number of unconnected elements present in the system. To increase simplicity in terms of minimizing diversity, each effect was connected with another event in a cause–effect unit formation (i.e., the instructor attributed causality for the high exam scores to a change in the format of his lectures and for his wife's actions to recent financial losses). To increase simplicity in terms of achieving maximum consistency between the elements of each unit formation, the events connected to the effects as causes were the events that were more consistent with the effects than were other events present in consciousness at that point in time. The instructor initially attributed causality for the high test scores to the change in lecture format rather than to some other event present in consciousness (e.g., his recent financial losses, the fact that his neighbor had a baby on the morning of the exam, the air conditioning) because the change in lectures was more consistent with the high test scores than were the other events. He initially attributed causality for his wife's behavior to his recent financial losses rather than to some other event present in consciousness (e.g., changing the format of his lectures, the argument over the condition of the lawn, the failure of his car to start that morning) because recent financial losses were more consistent with his wife's filing for divorce than were the other events. Furthermore, when presented with events (i.e., the error in grading and his wife's affections for another man) that were even more consistent with the effects than those that had first been seen as the cause, the instructor reattributed causality to the more consistent events.

To illustrate our approach to causal attribution, we have analyzed a hypothetical example in terms of the dynamics that we think govern the attribution process. Of course, the persuasiveness of this analysis is dependent on the reader's agreement with our intuitive assessment of the degrees of consistency among the various effects and the other events in the instructor's consciousness. In the following section, we present a more formal definition of our concept of consistency and discuss the general operation of that dynamic in causal attribution.

THE CONSISTENCY PRINCIPLE

First, our consistency principle deals with the degree of consistency between the properties of effects and other events. A property will be treated as any attribute of effects and events that either has magnitude or can otherwise be measured and represented dimensionally. For example, the position of effects and events in time is a property because it can be measured and represented dimensionally. The degree of affectivity associated with effects and events is also a property because affect has magnitude and can be represented dimensionally (i.e., magnitude of positive versus negative affect).

Second, we originally proposed (Duval & Hensley, 1976) that

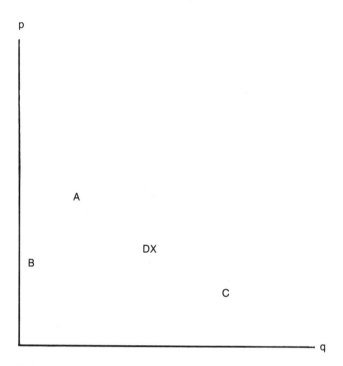

FIG. 1.1   Causal attribution as a function of similarity between effect event
X and possible causes *A, B, C,* and *D.*

the consistency principle applicable to the causal-attribution process refers to the degree of similarity between the properties of effects and properties of other events. As the degree of similarity
between the properties of an effect and another event increases,
the degree to which the effect and the event are consistent also increases. From this perspective, the tendency to maximize simplicity
in consciousness in terms of achieving maximum consistency
within unit formations would produce an attribution of causality
for a particular effect to that event with properties that are more
similar to those of the effect than are the properties of other events
present in consciousness. For example, let us assume that the person is aware of an effect *(X)* and several events *(A, B, C, D).* This
effect as well as all other events have properties *p* and *q.* In this
case the properties have magnitude. The effect has five units of *p*
and five units of *q.* The magnitude of the *p* and *q* properties
associated with the other events varies widely. This situation is il-

lustrated in Fig. 1.1. The effect and the events are represented as points on a two-dimensional plane. The dimensions are defined by the p and q properties of both the effect and the other events. The positions of the effect and the other events on this two-dimensional surface are determined by the magnitude of the p and q properties associated with each. The degree of similarity between the effect and each event is represented by the distance between their positions on the graph with decreasing distance indicating increasing similarity and vice versa. Strict application of the consistency principle to this situation predicts that causality for the effect will be attributed to the event with properties that are most similar to the properties of the effect in terms of the absolute distance between them (in this case, event D). If the situation includes two or more events that are equal in similarity to the effect on the p and q dimensions, application of the consistency principle predicts an equal tendency to attribute causality to each of those events.

The consistency principle as applied to causal attribution predicts that causality for an effect will be attributed to the event with properties that are more similar to the properties of that effect than are those of other events in consciousness. However, at this point, we must take the asymmetrical form of cause and effect structures into account. This asymmetry demands that events have certain features before they qualify as possible causes for particular effects. Because present application of the consistency principle is limited to processes that result in cause–effect unit formations, the following section discusses factors that determine which events qualify as possible causes for given effects.

THE ASYMMETRY CRITERIA

Tversky (1977) has identified two distinct types of relationships: symmetrical and asymmetrical. In symmetrical relationships, the elements are not rank ordered. $E = MC^2$ is an example of this type of relationship. E and MC^2 are treated as identities, and E does not follow from MC^2 to any greater extent than MC^2 follows from E. Asymmetrical relationships, on the other hand, involve elements that are rank ordered such that one (the variant) follows from the other (the prototype), but the reverse is not true. Tversky offers the relationship between father and son as an example of an asymmetrical relationship. The son (the variant) follows from the father (the prototype), but reversing the rank order between the two elements (the father follows from the son) seems odd or nonsensical. The relationship between a person's portrait and that actual person is similarly biased. The portrait (the variant) follows from the person (the prototype), but a reversal in this rank order (the person follows from the portrait) again seems odd or nonsensical.

Cause and effect relationships are clearly asymmetrical rather than symmetrical. The effect follows from the cause, whereas the reverse is not true. For example, we are at a party and hear a person say something nasty to a particular lady. The lady then faints. We believe that the nasty communication caused the woman to faint. Given this attribution, we would say that the physical act of fainting (the effect) followed from the nasty communication (the cause). We would not say that the communication (the cause) followed from the physical act of fainting (the effect). Similarly, if we are watching a game of pool and see the cue ball strike the eight ball which then moves toward the side pocket, we would say that the movement of the eight ball (the effect) followed from contact with the moving cue ball (the cause). We would not say that the movement of the cue ball followed from the movement of the eight ball (i.e., that the cause followed from the effect).

The asymmetry of cause and effect relationships implies that the elements connected in cause–effect unit formations must, to use Tversky's language, be related to one another as prototype and variant. The causal event must have the status of prototype; the effect event must have the status of variant, with prototype and variant representing a dichotomous variable (i.e., one that does not vary in degree). The existence of this asymmetry suggests that the set of events that could possibly be linked to a particular effect as a cause are limited to those events that meet at least two criteria. First, the events must possess some feature that causes them to have the status of prototype relative to the effect in question (i.e., the effect would follow from the events and not vice versa). Second, the events must not possess any other feature that causes them to have the status of variant relative to the effect. We refer to these two specifications as the asymmetry criteria.

For cause–effect unit formations, we suggest that the primary factor that determines whether events meet the first asymmetry criterion with regard to an effect involves the temporal relationship between the events and the effect. Events that happen before an effect occurs have the feature "preceded the effect in time," which causes them to have the status of prototype relative to the effect. Events that occur either after or at exactly the same time as the effect do not have this feature and do not have the status of prototype relative to the effect. For example, let us expand the previous situation involving the woman who faints at a cocktail party. In addition to the nasty communication and the physical collapse of the woman, let us assume that: (1) a man with whom she has had an affair arrives at the party before she faints; (2) the woman who faints does not normally drink alcoholic beverages but was persuaded to imbibe several martinis prior to fainting; (3) the woman is given smelling salts by an attendant after she faints; (4) a couple at the party become embroiled in an argument after the woman faints; (5) the woman drops her martini glass at exactly the same time as she faints. Under these circumstances, it seems clear that the temporal relationships between the various events and the effect (the fainting spell) determine which events have the status of prototype relative to the effect and which do not. The events that happened before the effect occurred (i.e., the nasty communication, the appearance of the ex-lover, and the ingestion of alcohol) have the status of prototype relative to the effect because the effect (the fainting) would follow from any of these events rather than vice versa. The events that happened after the effect occurred (i.e., the administration of the smelling salts and the couple's argument) or the event that happened at the same time as the effect (i.e., the dropping of the glass) do not have the status of prototype because the effect (the fainting) would not follow from events that succeeded it in time or occurred simultaneously. Put another way, it is conceivable that the fainting spell followed from the nasty communication, the appearance of the ex-lover, or the ingestion of alcohol. It is inconceivable that the fainting spell followed from the administration of the smelling salts, the couple's argument, or the dropping of the glass. (If anything, these latter events would follow from the fainting spell or, in the case of the dropped glass, would be in a symmetrical relationship to the effect.) Thus, only those events known (or assumed) to have happened before an effect occurs (i.e., previously occurring events) meet the first asymmetry criterion and qualify for inclusion in the set of possible causes for that effect.

Of the set of events that happen prior to the occurrence of an effect, those events having properties with magnitudes equal to or greater than the magnitude of the properties belonging to the effect also meet the second asymmetry criterion. They do not have any feature that causes them to have the status of a variant relative to the effect. Previously occurring events with properties that are lesser in magnitude than the properties of the effect do not meet this second criterion and would not qualify as possible causes for that effect. This hypothesis is based on Tversky's (1977) examination of noncausal asymmetrical relationships, which indicates that inequality in the magnitude of properties shared by different stimuli affects the prototype-variant status of those stimuli. For example, if the magnitude of a property associated with two different stimuli is unequal, the lesser of the two stimuli will tend to be seen as a variant of the greater. Thus, a less saturated color of red is seen as a variant of the more saturated red.

Applying this inequality effect to events with common properties that differ in magnitude suggests that events of lesser magnitude would have the status of variant relative to events of greater magnitude. For example, suppose we walk into a room and see a roaring fire in the fireplace and a small ember on the floor. According to the inequality effect, we should see the ember as a variant of the fire (i.e., the ember follows from the fire rather than vice versa) because the magnitude of the ember is less than that of the fire with regard to properties shared by both (e.g., heat emitted, brightness).

Within the context of cause–effect unit formation, the inequality effect suggests that previously occurring events with properties that are lesser in magnitude than the properties of the effect violate the second asymmetry criterion. They have the feature "lesser in magnitude than the effect," which causes them to have the status of variant relative to the effect. Events with properties that are equal to or greater in magnitude than the properties associated with the effect would not have this feature. Thus, only those previously occurring events with properties that are equal to or greater in magnitude than those of the effect meet both asymmetry criteria and qualify as possible causes for the effect.

Evidence supporting this hypothesis is found in Michotte's research. In one set of Michotte's (1963) experiments on perceived causality, the subject saw a rectangle (A) approaching a second and stationary rectangle (B). A then made contact with B, stopped, and B moved off in the same direction that A had been moving. Subjects observed this sequence of events several times. One set of experimental variations consisted in changing the speed of A's approach toward B and the speed of B's departure from A. When A's approach speed was either equal to or greater than the speed of B's movement away from A, subjects formed the clear impression that A's motion and contact with B caused B's movement. However, if the speed of B's movement after contact with A was greater than A's approach speed, subjects consistently reported that A's movement and contact with B was not the direct cause of B's movement. From the present point of view, these results reflect the operation of the second asymmetry criterion. When the magnitude of the previously occurring event (the speed of A's movement toward B) was less than the magnitude of the effect (the speed of B's movement away from A), the previously occurring event had the feature "lesser in magnitude than the effect," and this caused it to have the status of variant relative to the effect. This feature violated the second asymmetry criterion and led to a rejection of the previously occurring event (A's movement) as a possible cause of the effect (B's movement), even though A's movement preceded B's movement in time. On the other hand, when the magnitude of the previously occurring event (A's movement) was either equal to or greater than the magnitude of the effect, the previously occurring event did not have any feature that violated the second asymmetry criterion. Under these circumstances, A's movement was accepted as a possible cause for the effect and was, for reasons we discuss in Chapter 2, linked with the effect in a cause–effect unit formation.

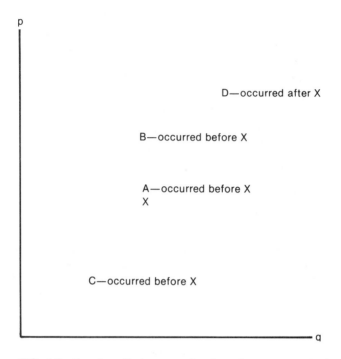

FIG. 1.2   Causal attribution as a function of asymmetry criteria and similarity between effect event X and possible causes A, B, C, and D.

We have argued that the asymmetry of cause and effect relationships limits the set of events qualifying as possible causes to those events that: (1) are known (or assumed) to have occurred before an effect occurred; (2) have properties that are equal to or greater in magnitude than the magnitude of the properties belonging to an effect. Application of the consistency principle to the set of events that qualify as possible causes for any effect is straightforward. Causality will be attributed to the possible cause with properties that are more similar to the properties of the effect than are those of other possible causes. To return to our previous example, let us assume that a person is aware of an effect (X) and other events (A, B, C, and D). Events A, B, and C occur before the effect; D occurs after the effect. The effect and each of the events have properties p and q. The magnitude of these properties, for p and q respectively, are: X, 5 and 5; A, 6 and 5; B, 7 and 5; C, 3 and 4; D, 8 and 8. This situation is presented graphically in Fig. 1.2. Under these conditions, the asymmetry criteria limit the events that qualify as possible causes for the effect to A and B. Event D occurs after the effect, and the magnitude of C's properties are less than the magnitude of the properties associated with the effect. From this set of possible causes, the consistency principle predicts that attribution of causality for the effect will be to A because A's properties are more similar to the properties of X than are those of B. If the situation includes two or more previously occurring events that are equal in similarity to the effect on the p and q dimensions, the consistency principle predicts an equal tendency to attribute causality to each of those events.

ATTRIBUTION AND COGNITION

The theory of causal attribution presented thus far is based on the degree of consistency among the properties of effects and events that qualify as possible causes. In this formulation, the term *properties* refers to properties of the internal neural representations or experienced correlates of external stimulus events. Research concerning cognitive processes (Gregory, 1970) makes this position necessary by showing that all external stimulus events and other stimuli are first translated: "into the language of the brain, and reconstituted into experience of the surrounding [world] [p. 7]." Although these processes of translation are not completely understood, the fact that the external is translated into the internal suggests that any process of cognitive organization, including causal attribution, must deal with the properties of the products of the translation rather than working directly on the properties of the external world. In social psychology, the products of this external-to-internal translation are typically referred to as cognitions or cognized events (objects, situations, etc.).

Because cognition involves translation of the external into the internal, we assume that the properties of cognized effects and events that may qualify as possible causes are a function of two factors: (1) properties associated with the external stimulus events that form the referents of the cognitions; (2) properties of the internal systems that mediate or participate in the process of translating the external stimulus events into cognitions. That properties of external stimulus events (e.g., position in time and space) contribute to the properties of the cognitions of those events is self-evident. Phenomena indicating that some internal system affects the properties of cognized events, objects, etc., support the notion that internal systems contribute to the properties of cognized effects and events that may qualify as possible causes. The contrast-shift effect is an excellent example of these phenomena.

In research concerning the contrast-shift effect, people judge, for example, the weight of a particular test stimulus. If the person has previously experienced an "anchor" stimulus that is considerably heavier or lighter than the test stimulus, the judged value of the test stimulus is shifted in a direction opposite to the value of the anchor stimulus. A person who has picked up a heavy anchor stimulus judges the value of the test stimulus to be lighter than does a person who has picked up a light anchor stimulus, although the actual weight of the test stimulus is the same for both persons. This contrast-shift effect has been obtained with regard to a variety of dimensions (e.g., length, color, brightness, similarity, affective intensity). Furthermore, a series of experiments by Dawes and his associates (1972) and the documentation of contrast-shift effects in classical conditioning (Grings, Givens, & Carey, 1979) indicate that these differences in the judged value of the test stimulus represent real differences in the cognized properties of the test stimulus rather than category expansion (Upshaw, 1968). These findings imply that the contrast-shift effect occurs because the properties of some internal system that mediates or participates in the translation of stimuli into cognition affects the properties of the stimuli as they are represented in consciousness.

The existence of the contrast-shift effect (as well as other phenomena in which the properties of the cognized object or event do not bear an exact one-to-one correspondence to the properties of the external stimulus or stimulus event) supports our contention that the properties of cognized effects and possible causes are affected by the properties of internal systems. This position is incorporated as a formal proposition of the theory. The consistency principle and the asymmetry criteria apply to the properties of cognized effects and events. These properties are a function of the properties of external stimulus events themselves and the properties of those cognitive and affective systems that mediate or participate in the translation of the external world into cognition. We should point out that the plausibility of this position is not necessarily challenged by the naive individual's failure or inability to recognize that the properties of cognized effects and other events are influenced by properties of internal systems as well as by those of external stimulus events. In fact, Nisbett and Wilson (1977) argue convincingly that people are not typically aware of the factors that actually influence their behavior, cognitive or otherwise. We think that this conclusion would be particularly true when the factors are properties of internal systems that mediate or participate in the translation of external stimulus events into cognitions.

To summarize, we have presented a theory of causal attribution based on consciousness as a dynamic process that moves to maximize simplicity within its boundaries. In pursuit of this goal, consciousness connects cognitions of effects and events that qualify as possible causes for these effects in cause–effect unit formations such that consistency between connected cognitions is maximal. Consistency is defined in terms of degree of similarity between the properties of cognized effects and possible causes. The asymmetry criteria determine whether an event qualifies as a possible cause for a given effect. The properties of cognized effects and events that may qualify as possible causes are a function of properties of external stimulus events that form referents for cognitions and properties of cognitive and affective systems that mediate or participate in the translation of external stimulus events into cognitions. This theory generates one major hypothesis. Given any cognized effect, a person will attribute causality to the cognized possible cause that is more consistent with the effect than are other possible causes. We assume that this hypothesis holds true regardless of the particular properties of cognized effects and possible causes being considered. In Chapters 2 through 6 we apply this hypothesis to the temporal, spatial, focal, and affective dimensions of cognition.

2 Time and Space

Each cognized effect and event that may qualify as a possible cause for an effect has a position in time, a position in space, and positions on other dimensions (e.g., affectivity and focalization). To qualify as a possible cause, an event must happen before an effect occurs and must be equal to or greater in magnitude than the effect on other dimensions. This chapter focuses on the relationship between the temporal and spatial positions of possible causes and effects and causal attribution. To simplify exposition, the term *cognized* is not used when referring to effects and possible causes until the latter part of the chapter.

The consistency principle suggests that causality for some effect will be attributed to the possible cause that is most similar to the effect on all dimensions. To see how this principle applies to the temporal and spatial dimensions, let us conceptualize time and space in terms of a two-dimensional surface with the horizontal dimension representing time and the vertical representing space. Now we place three events (A, B, and X) on this two-dimensional surface in terms of their time and place of occurrence (Fig. 2.1). The temporal and spatial similarity among these events is computed in terms of the horizontal and vertical distances between the particular positions of each event. In Fig. 2.1, the horizontal distance between A and X is less than that between B and X. Thus,

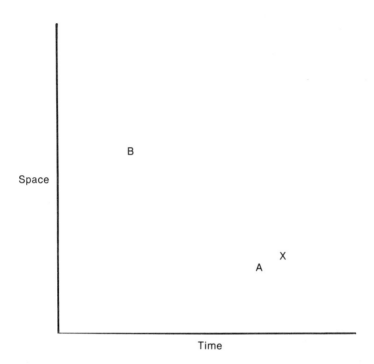

FIG. 2.1   Causal attribution as a function of temporal and spatial similarity.

A and X are more similar to each other on the dimension of time than are B and X. The vertical distance between A and X is also less than that between B and X. Thus, A is more similar to X than B is in terms of their positions in space. Now let us assume that X represents an effect (a mild attack of anxiety experienced by Tom). A and B represent two possible causes for the effect (i.e., events occurring before the effect that have magnitudes equal to or greater than the magnitude of the effect on other shared dimensions). B is a conversation between Joe and Sally that Tom overheard from a distance 30 minutes before the anxiety attack occurred. A is a conversation that Tom had with Sam three minutes before the anxiety attack occurred. There are no other possible causes for the effect present in the situation. Application of the consistency principle predicts that causality for X (the anxiety attack) will be attributed to A (the conversation with Sam) rather than *B* (the conversation overheard between Joe and Sally) because the occurrences of the talk with Sam and the anxiety attack are more similar to each other on the dimensions of time and space than are the occurrences of the overheard conversation and the anxiety attack (all other factors held constant). If we introduce a third possible cause that is closer to *X* in time and space than is either *A* or *B* (e.g., Tom talks with Bill one minute before the anxiety attack), attribution of causality for *X* to this event should occur. If two or more potential causes are equally similar to the effect on the time and space dimensions (two firecrackers explode at the same time and distance from Tom), there should be an equal tendency to attribute causality to each of those events.

Michotte's (1963) well-known research concerning the impact of time and space on causal attribution is compatible with application of the consistency principle to these dimensions. In one set of experiments, for example, Michotte varied the interval between the point in time when a moving rectangle (*A*) made contact with a stationary rectangle (*B*) and the point in time when *B* began to move away from *A*. As this interval decreased, the tendency to perceive *B*'s movement as caused by *A* increased and vice versa. From the present point of view, Michotte was varying the degree of temporal similarity between an effect (*B*'s movement) and a possible cause for that effect (*A*'s movement and contact with *B*) while holding the degree of temporal similarity between the effect and other possible causes (e.g., intervention by the experimenter) constant. As the elapsed time between the occurrence of *B*'s movement and the possible cause decreased, the temporal similarity between the two events increased, while the degree of temporal similarity between the effect and other possible causes remained constant. Increasing the temporal similarity between *A*'s movement and contact with *B* and *B*'s movement away from *A* increased the probability that the possible cause represented by *A* was more similar to the effect on the dimension of time than were other possible causes. As predicted by application of the consistency principle to the dimension of time, increasing this probability increased the tendency to attribute causality for *B*'s movement to *A*. If subjects were asked to determine the cause for *B*'s movement, given the option of attributing causality to a possible cause that occurred either just before *B* began moving or that happened ten seconds before *B*'s movement began, the effect of temporal similarity on causal attribution would be even clearer. Provided that all other factors were held constant, subjects would undoubtedly attribute causality to the possible cause that occurred just prior to the effect because, in the present terminology, that possible cause would be more similar to the effect than would other possible causes with regard to the temporal dimension.

Results from a second set of studies (Michotte, 1963), which varied the spatial proximity of a possible cause and an effect, support application of the consistency principle to the dimension of space. The temporal interval between the occurrence of the possible cause (rectangle *A* moving toward rectangle *B* and stopping) and the effect (*B*'s movement away from *A*) was brief and held constant for all conditions. Spatial proximity of the two events was manipulated by varying the distance between *B*'s initial position and the point where *A*'s movement toward *B* stopped. As this distance decreased, the tendency to see *A*'s movement as the cause of *B*'s movement increased and vice versa. In this case, the experimental manipulations varied the degree of spatial similarity between the occurrences of an effect and a possible cause while holding the degree of spatial similarity between the effect and other possible causes constant. Decreasing the distance between the points in space where the occurrence of the possible cause (*A*'s movement) ended and the occurrence of the effect (*B*'s movement) began increased the spatial similarity between the two events, while the degree of spatial similarity between the effect and other possible causes remained constant. As similarity on this dimension increased, the probability that *A*'s movement was more similar to *B*'s movement than were other possible causes also increased. As this probability increased, the tendency to attribute causality for *B*'s movement to *A* increased. The same effect would be obtained in a forced choice situation. If a person were given the option of attributing causality to a possible cause that occurred in close spatial proximity to an effect versus one that occurred some distance away, attribution would be directed to the possible cause that was most similar to the effect on the spatial dimension (all other factors held constant).

TEMPORAL SIMILARITY
AND COVARIATION OVER TIME

Applied to the dimension of time, the covariation principle (Kelley, 1967) predicts that an effect will be attributed to a possible cause that is present when the effect is present and absent when the effect is absent. This hypothesis is typically tested by telling subjects that a given effect (e.g., John laughs) either almost always occurs shortly after a possible cause for the effect occurs (e.g., the comedian tells jokes) or almost never occurs shortly after the possible cause (e.g., John almost never laughs after the comedian tells jokes). The possible cause and effect are said to covary over time to a greater extent in the first case than in the second. The covariation principle predicts a stronger tendency to attribute causality for the effect to the possible cause as temporal covariation between the two events increases.

A substantial amount of research supports the temporal covariation hypothesis. Under conditions of high temporal covariation (e.g., John almost always laughs at the comedian's jokes, likes a movie, insults another person), people tend to attribute the effect (i.e., John's behavior or feelings) to the possible cause (i.e., something about the comedian, the movie, the person). Under conditions of low temporal covariation (e.g., an effect almost never happens after the possible cause occurs), people tend not to attribute causality for the effect to the possible cause (McArthur, 1972).

From our perspective, the effect of temporal covariation on causal attribution reflects the operation of the consistency principle. This conclusion is based on the following analysis. The degree of temporal similarity between an effect and a possible cause for that effect is high when the effect occurs shortly after the possible cause. The degree of temporal similarity is low when the effect does not occur shortly after the possible cause. As operationalized in the relevant literature, all statements concerning temporal covariation contain information implying that effects and possible causes are high in temporal similarity on some occasions (e.g., John laughs shortly after hearing the comedian's jokes) but low on other occasions (e.g., John does not laugh shortly after hearing the comedian's jokes). Manipulation of temporal covariation consists in varying the frequency with which the separate occurrences of effects and possible causes are either high or low in temporal similarity. Under conditions of high temporal covariation, the degree of temporal similarity between the occurrences of effects and possible causes is almost always high and rarely low (e.g., John almost always laughs shortly after the comedian's jokes). Under conditions of low temporal covariation, the degree of temporal similarity between the occurrences of the effects and possible causes is almost always low and rarely high (e.g., John almost never laughs shortly after the comedian's jokes). If the model of judgmental processes involving inconsistent information (Anderson, 1965) is applied to these two conditions, we see that the average degree of temporal similarity between effects and possible

TABLE 2.1
A Consistency-Similarity Explanation of the Covariation Phenomenon

High Temporal Covariation Condition

Situation:

John almost always laughs at the comedian's jokes.

Analysis:		Degree of Temporal Similarity on Each Occasion	Average Degree of Temporal Similarity
	4 comedian—laughter	high	
	3 comedian—no laughter	low	
Occasions	2 comedian—laughter	high	high
	1 comedian—laughter	high	
	Time		

Low Temporal Covariation Condition

Situation:

John almost never laughs at the comedian's jokes.

Analysis:		Degree of Temporal Similarity on Each Occasion	Average Degree of Temporal Similarity
	4 comedian—no laughter	low	
	3 comedian—laughter	high	
Occasions	2 comedian—no laughter	low	low
	1 comedian—no laughter	low	
	Time		

causes is greater under conditions of high as opposed to low temporal covariation (see Table 2.1). Inasmuch as a high (or low) degree of temporal similarity between an effect and a possible cause increases (or decreases) the probability that the cause is more similar to the effect than are other possible causes (Michotte, 1963), a high or low degree of temporal similarity averaged over occasions should have the same impact. Thus, covariation can be interpreted as a consistency effect. Increasing the degree of temporal covariation between effects and possible causes increases the tendency to attribute causality to those causes by increasing the probability that they are more similar to the effects on the dimension of time than are other possible causes. Decreasing the degree of temporal covariation decreases the tendency to attribute causality to those possible causes by decreasing the probability that those causes are more similar to the effects on the dimension of time than are other possible causes.

In addition to providing a dynamic basis for the effect of time and space on causal attribution, applying the consistency principle to the temporal and spatial positions of possible causes and effects further defines the nature and scope of the influence of these variables in the attribution process. For example, from Kelley's point of view (Kelley, 1973), temporal covariation is indeterminate unless there are multiple observations of the temporal relationships between possible causes and effects. The present approach implies that the degree of temporal similarity between an effect and a possible cause influences causal attribution even when information is limited to a single observation of the two events. For example, the knowledge that John laughed two seconds after a joke, as opposed to 20 minutes after a joke, should affect the tendency to attribute John's laughter to the joke even though this knowledge is based on only one observation. Of course, multiple observations could increase confidence in any attribution of causality by increasing certainty that the temporal sequence and relationship between the effect and possible cause were perceived correctly. In addition, multiple exposures to an effect event and a possible cause could increase the tendency to see the two events as causally related by increasing the probability that the observer notices the particular degree of temporal similarity between the two events.

Kelley's covariation principle is also tied to the concept of temporal contiguity. If an effect event is always (or almost always) temporally contiguous with a possible cause, the two events will be seen as cause and effect. If the occurrence of the effect is never (or almost never) temporally contiguous with a possible cause, there will be no impression of causality. In contrast to this approach, we assume that the degree of temporal similarity between effects and possible causes influences causal attribution even in the absence of temporal contiguity. If a possible cause for an effect (A) occurs five minutes before the effect but is more similar to the effect on the dimension of time than are other possible causes, causality for the effect should be attributed to A even though A's occurrence and that of the effect are not temporally contiguous.

Finally, our approach identifies spatial similarity as an important variable in causal attribution. This point becomes particularly important when two possible causes are equally similar to an effect on the temporal dimension but differ from the effect on the spatial dimension. For example, Testa (1975) varied the degree of physical proximity between a conditioned stimulus (i.e., lights) and an unconditioned stimulus (i.e., air blasts) while holding the temporal interval between the onset of the two events constant. He found that increasing physical proximity between the CS and the UCS decreased the number of trials to conditioned suppression of responding, an effect he attributed to the impact of spatial proximity (i.e., similarity) on the formation of cause–effect units.

Although temporal and spatial similarity appear to be fundamental variables in the causal-attribution process, their role in mediating social psychological phenomena has not always been recognized. In the following section, we discuss data suggesting that the effort-justification effect is a causal-attribution phenomenon mediated by temporal similarity.

AN ATTRIBUTIONAL ANALYSIS OF
THE EFFORT-JUSTIFICATION EFFECT

There is a substantial amount of research showing that individuals who voluntarily engage or expect to engage in unpleasant activity in order for some second event to occur (e.g., attainment of group membership, Aronson & Mills, 1959; listening to a persuasive communication, Wicklund, Cooper, & Linder, 1967) evaluate the second event more positively than do individuals who do not engage or expect to engage in such activity. This effect is called *effort justification* and is typically explained in terms of cognitive dissonance theory (Festinger, 1957). To justify voluntary participation in the unpleasant activity, people value the second event more positively; as the magnitude of the unpleasantness associated with the first activity increases, the positive evaluation of the second event increases in degree (Aronson & Mills, 1959).

Despite the impressiveness of the effort-justification literature, there would seem to be instances in which aversive activity or conditions (i.e., noxious stimulation) lower rather than raise the evaluation of the following event. For instance, undergoing an unpleasant initiation ritual in order to gain membership in a group may increase positive evaluation of that group. On the other hand, imagine a person's reaction if the unpleasant activities or conditions began just prior to group membership and persisted as long as membership continued. This onset and continuation of noxious stimulation would probably decrease rather than increase the person's liking for the group.

The differences between situations that elevate and those that might depress evaluation of the following target event seem to involve the timing of the onset–offset of noxious stimulation and the occurrence of the target event. This suggests that the effort-justification effect may be an attributional phenomenon mediated by temporal similarity. For example, in research concerning the effort-justification effect, the termination of actual or anticipated noxious stimulation occurs shortly before the second event occurs (e.g., gaining group membership). Under these conditions the consistency principle applied to the dimension of time suggests that causality for the occurrence of the second event (the effect or target event) would tend to be attributed to the termination of noxious stimulation. However, the termination of noxious stimulation is a pleasant event, and attribution of causality for the occurrence of the target event to a pleasant event should increase the positive evaluation of the target event. From this perspective, the effort-justification effect (i.e., increased positive evaluation of a target event following offset of noxious stimulation) is an attributional rather than a dissonance-reduction phenomenon.

If the effort-justification effect is an attributional phenomenon mediated by the temporal relationship between the various events involved, it should be possible to reverse the effect by changing the temporal relationship between events. Specifically, if the onset of noxious stimulation occurs shortly before the target event occurs and continues for the duration of that event, the person should attribute causality for the occurrence of the target event to the noxious event. This attribution should result in devaluation of the target event just as attribution of causality for the target event to a positive event (i.e., termination of noxious stimulation) results in a more positive evaluation of the target event. Dissonance theory would not predict differences in evaluation of the target event as a function of the temporal relationships between the onset or offset of noxious stimulation and the occurrence of the target event.

In order to compare the causal-attribution interpretation of the effort-justification effect with the cognitive dissonance approach, we exposed subjects to onset of, offset of, or no noxious stimulation prior to their hearing a 10-minute tape recording of everyday sounds (e.g., a door closing, footsteps). The procedure used in one condition replicated the sequence of events in the standard effort-justification experiment. The noxious stimulation was terminated 1 minute before the tape was presented (offset condition). In a second condition, the noxious stimulation began about 1 to 3 minutes before the tape was played and continued throughout the tape (onset condition). In a control condition subjects were not exposed to any noxious stimulation. Under these conditions, the attributional approach predicts that subjects in the offset condition would rate the tape more positively than those in the control condition. Subjects in the onset condition, however, should rate the tape more negatively than those in the control condition. Cognitive dissonance theory predicts that subjects in the onset and offset conditions would rate the tape more positively than subjects in the control condition, and no differences between the onset and offset conditions should be observed.

The choice of noxious stimulation was determined by three considerations. First, it was necessary to minimize distraction for those subjects who would be listening to the tape while they were still experiencing the noxious stimulation. Second, it was necessary to continue the noxious stimulation over a substantial period of time without any danger to the subjects' welfare. Third, it was necessary to be able to predict with some accuracy when the stimulation would become noxious. In pretesting, we found that wrapping subjects in a heavy blanket in a warm room (85°) and requiring them to sit up straight and very still in a hardback chair satisfied these requirements. These conditions were minimally distracting although mildly noxious, and the mean time delay between commencement of this procedure and subjects' self-reports of the first real discomfort was fairly predictable ($M = 9.6$ minutes with a standard deviation of 1.89).

Thirty-nine male and female undergraduates volunteered to participate in this study and were randomly assigned to the three conditions. Subjects were run individually by a female experimenter. The experimenter began by telling subjects that they were participating in a study designed to determine the relationship between external skin temperature and electrodermal responses to external stimuli. After providing a convincing rationale for doing the study, the experimenter attached electrodes to the subject's hand and upper arm to measure galvanic skin responses (GSR) and external skin temperature. In the experimental conditions, the experimenter indicated that this test required raising the subjects' external skin temperature considerably above normal and then exposing them to an external stimulus (viz., a tape recording). They were told that their GSR responses to this stimulus would then be measured. At this point, subjects were asked if they wished to participate in the experiment and were told that they would receive full credit even if they chose not to continue. All subjects agreed to participate.

In the offset condition, the experimenter wrapped a heavy blanket around each subject saying that it would take about 10 minutes to raise his or her external skin temperature to the desired level. She instructed subjects to sit up straight, close their eyes, and remain as still as possible to insure accurate recording of their GSR responses. She concluded by saying that the blanket would be removed after their skin temperature had reached the desired level and that they could then relax and listen to the tape recording. She again stated that their GSR responses to the tape would be measured while they listened. In the onset condition, subjects received identical instructions with the following exceptions: They would remain wrapped in the blanket and would have to remain as still as possible throughout the experiment. Subjects in the control condition received the same rationale for the experimental procedure, but the raising of their external skin temperature was not mentioned; they were told that there would be a 10-minute wait while their external skin temperature stabilized.

After subjects in the experimental conditions had been wrapped in the blanket, the experimenter busied herself with paper work. In the offset condition, the experimenter waited 10.5 minutes and removed the blanket; 1 minute later, she presented the tape recording. In the onset condition, the experimenter waited for 11.5 minutes and played the tape recording. In the control condition, subjects sat quietly but comfortably for 11.5 minutes; then the experimenter played the tape.

After playing a 10-minute tape recording of doors opening and closing, footsteps, and the like, the experimenter removed the blanket for onset subjects, told them they could relax, and left the room for 5 minutes to allow the physiological condition of the onset subjects to return to normal. The experimenter also left the room for 5 minutes in the offset and control conditions. For all conditions, she justified her behavior by saying that she had to get some questionnaires for the subjects to fill out. The experimenter then returned and asked the subjects to answer a few questions about their subjective impressions of the tape so that each person's individual reactions could be taken into account when interpreting the GSR data.

At this point, the experimenter administered the dependent measures, which asked subjects to rate the taped sounds on three dimensions: the extent to which the sounds were pleasant–unpleasant, interesting–boring, and enjoyable–unenjoyable for the subjects. Each item was accompanied by a 16-point scale anchored with the appropriate positive and negative labels. As a check on the noxious-stimulation manipulation, subjects also rated how

TABLE 2.2
Mean Ratings of Physical Comfort

	Offset	*Onset*	*Control*
M	9.69_a	5.17_c	7.96_b

Note: As mean values decrease, rated discomfort increases. Means that do not share common subscripts differ significantly.
$n = 13$ for each condition.

TABLE 2.3
Mean Evaluation of the Tape Recording

	Offset	*Onset*	*Control*
M	27.50_a	18.65_c	22.62_b

Note: As mean values increase, positiveness of evaluation increases. Means that do not share common subscripts differ significantly.
$n = 13$ for each condition.

comfortable they had felt while listening to the tape by marking the appropriate point on a 16-point scale labeled *very uncomfortable* and *very comfortable* at the end points.

On a conceptual level, the procedures used in this experiment were designed to create conditions in which the occurrence of the target event (listening to taped sounds) was preceded by either a pleasant event (offset of noxious stimulation) or an unpleasant event (onset of noxious stimulation). We expected subjects to attribute causality for the target event to the pleasant or unpleasant experience that immediately preceded it. This should increase or decrease subjects' liking for the tape relative to that of the control group, which experienced neither the pleasant nor the unpleasant event prior to hearing the tape. These predictions were supported. First, the manipulation of onset and offset of aversive stimulation was successful (see Table 2.2). Subjects in the onset condition reported feeling considerably more uncomfortable while listening to the tape than did control subjects; subjects in the offset condition reported feeling more comfortable while listening to the tape than did control subjects. Second, an analysis of subjects' ratings of the taped sounds (see Table 2.3; correlations among the three dependent measures ranged from $r = .52$ to .70 and were summed for analysis) indicates that ratings in the offset condition were more positive than in the control condition ($p < .05$), a finding that replicates the typical effort-justification effect. However, subjects' ratings of the taped sounds were more negative in the onset than in the control condition ($p < .05$), a finding that definitely favors an attributional interpretation of the effort-justification effect with temporal similarity as the critical variable determining causal attribution.

Although these results support the idea that the effort-justification effect is an attributional phenomenon mediated by the temporal relationship between a pleasant or an unpleasant event and a second event (e.g., listening to the taped sounds, gaining group membership), some results reported in the literatue appear to be inconsistent with this analysis. For example, in a study by Gerard and Mathewson (1966), subjects in the aversive stimulation-control condition experienced offset of an electric shock prior to hearing a group discussion. These subjects did not evaluate the group discussion as positively as did experimental subjects who also experienced offset of an electric shock before hearing the group discussion. The only difference between the two conditions involved instructions concerning the relationship between enduring the electric shock and gaining group membership. However, it does not appear that these instructions produced differences between the two groups in terms of the actual time interval between offset of the aversive stimulation and hearing the group discussion. Given no differences in the actual time interval that separated termination of aversive stimulation and the occurrence of the target event, why didn't subjects in the aversive stimulation-control condition attribute as much causality for the group discussion to the offset of the stimulation and rate it as positively as did subjects in the experimental condition? Second, although past effort-justification research fails to report the time delay between offset of aversive stimulation and the occurrence of the target event, it is evident that the interval is longer than the 1–3 minute delay used in our experiment. Increasing the time interval between the occurrence of a possible cause (e.g., termination of aversive stimulation) and the occurrence of an effect (e.g., gaining group membership) increases the probability that another possible cause will be more similar to the effect. This possibility also suggests that the effort-justification effect may not be mediated by causal attribution. On the other hand, these apparent inconsistencies between present theory and past research may be resolved by considering the distinction between the external and the experienced time interval that separates events.

In reviewing effort-justification research, we find that subjects are typically told that the aversive stimulation will be followed by a second event (the effect). Given these instructions, it is possible that subjects subjectively experience the occurrence of the effect immediately after termination of the first unpleasant event. In Aronson and Mills' (1959) severity of initiation study, for example, subjects may have assumed that the effect (i.e., attainment of group membership) occurred immediately after termination of the unpleasant initiation procedure, even though they had not at that time actually participated in the group. That is to say, in the subject's mind the degree of temporal similarity between offset of the noxious stimulation and attainment of group membership may have been quite high although the actual offset-to-group participation time interval was substantial. This conclusion suggests that the subjectively experienced degree of temporal similarity between the offset of noxious stimulation and the occurrence of a target event is the critical variable affecting causal attribution in effort-justification research—a factor that, in the Aronson and Mills (1959) study, led subjects to attribute causality for the attainment of group membership to the offset of aversive stimulation and thereby increased the positiveness of their evaluation of the group.

This proposition can also be applied to Gerard and Mathewson's (1966) results. Unlike subjects in the experimental conditions, subjects in the aversive stimulation-control condition of that experiment were not told that the group discussion would follow the offset of shock. Without this information, the subjectively experienced time interval between offset of shock and hearing the discussion should be equivalent to the amount of time that actually separated the two events. Because the events were separated in real time, temporal similarity between the occurrence of each event would be low. This would decrease the aversive stimulation-control subject's tendency to attribute the cause for the group discussion to the offset of shock (a pleasant experience) and, thus, reduce any tendency to evaluate the group discussion more positively.

In interpreting some of the apparent inconsistencies between our approach and the results of previous effort-justification research, we have essentially proposed that the critical temporal factor in causal attribution is the degree of experienced temporal similarity between the points in time at which cognitions of events occur in consciousness. This position is a logical extension of our basic approach: The organization of attributional processes operates on cognitions of events (i.e., the internal representations of events) rather than on the external referents of those cognitions. Although the temporal similarity between the cognitions of events may often coincide with the external, "clock" time interval that separates those events, it is the internal interval separating the cognitions of events that determines the degree of temporal similarity between those cognized events and thus the tendency to link them in cause–effect unit formations. This conceptualization of the causal-attribution process further differentiates our approach from the concept of covariation over time. That is to say, temporal similarity between the cognition of events will influence causal attribution even when the external time interval between the actual occurrences of those events is substantial. An experiment by Duval, Duval, and Neely (1979) illustrates this point.

Strictly speaking, the present approach implies that one could induce a person to attribute causality for an effect to any possible cause by artificially introducing the cognition of that cause immediately before introducing the cognition of the effect, regardless of the external, objective temporal similarity between the two events (other factors held constant). In order to test this hypothesis, we exposed subjects to their live images on a TV monitor for 1 minute. Subjects then saw a videotape concerning victims of venereal disease. This manipulation should have made the cognition of self and the cognition of the effect (the plight of VD victims) temporally similar (as well as spatially proximate) to one another. In a control condition, subjects were exposed to their image for a 1-minute period 5 minutes before seeing the tape of VD victims. Attribution of responsibility to self for the victims' welfare was then measured. (Asking the question in terms of causality would have made little sense.) As predicted, subjects who saw their image immediately before being exposed to the video-tape attributed more responsibility to self for the welfare of VD victims than did subjects who experienced a 4-minute interval between seeing their own image and exposure to the tape. This result was replicated using poverty-stricken Latin Americans as the target group. Therefore, the time interval and, by implication, the spatial interval that affect causal attribution appear to be subjectively based rather than based on some measure external to the individual's experience.

3 Focal Consciousness

A discussion of the way in which the present theoretical approach is applied to the temporal and spatial properties of cognized effects and possible causes was presented in the previous chapter. In Chapter 1, we proposed that properties of internal systems, which mediate or participate in the translation of distal stimulus events into cognized effects and events that may qualify as possible causes, also contribute to the properties of those cognitions. In this chapter, we discuss contributions of focal consciousness to cognized stimuli and stimulus events and how these contributions influence the attribution process.

SUBSTANTIALITY AND FOCAL CONSCIOUSNESS

It seems clear that there is a dimension of cognition that is defined by the substantiality of internal representations of the external world. For example, my cognition of a tragedy that befell a friend is more substantial and "stands out" in consciousness to a greater extent than cognitions of more mundane occurrences. Or during a drive through the country, I point out a particular pastoral scene to my traveling companion. Over lunch, I begin to discuss that scene because it stands out in my mind to a greater extent than other things seen that day. But it shortly becomes clear that my friend's cognition of that scene does not have a similar status within his consciousness. He wants to talk about a piece of farm machinery that he pointed out to me, but which I can barely recall. Of course, this dimension of cognition could be a function of properties of the stimulus referents for the cognitions. The tragedy as an external stimulus event could have properties, which are lacking or present to a lesser extent in more mundane occurrences, that caused it to be impressed on my consciousness. The village scene that stands out in my mind could have had properties unnoticed by my friend that caused the situation to be impressed on my consciousness, with the reverse being true for the farm machinery. However, we find that the substantiality of cognitions with similar external referents can differ. The cognition of our wedding ceremony seems more substantial and stands out in our consciousnesses more than our cognition of an acquaintance's wedding ceremony, although an uninvolved observer would probably describe the two situations as having similar properties. We also find that the substantiality of cognitions with differing external referents can be quite similar. Our cognitions of a concert by Horowitz and of the Arc de Triomphe seem to be equally substantial and stand out in consciousness to a similar degree even though the properties of their stimulus referents are quite different. These examples suggest that the substantiality of internal representations is contributed, at least in part, by some internal mediational system. Specifically, we (Duval & Hensley, 1976) have proposed the following model: (1) consciousness mediates the translation of all external stimuli into cognition; (2) consciousness consists of two separate systems, which we have called *focal* and *nonfocal*; (3) to the extent (duration x intensity) that a stimulus is processed in focal consciousness, the substantiality of the internal representation (i.e., cognition) of that stimulus will increase. The operation of this model is illustrated in the following example.

Two people are confronted by the same problem. One person pays little attention to it. The second worries about it (processes it in focal consciousness) intensely and for long periods of time. At some later point, the person who has worried about the problem appears to have "blown it out of proportion" or "made a mountain out of a molehill'' relative to the person who has not worried. From the present point of view, these differences between the individuals' perceptions of the problem are not due to differences in the inherent properties of the problem. They are due to differences in the extent to which each person processed the problem in focal consciousness. The problem is greater for the worrier than for the nonworrier because the worrier's concentration of focal consciousness on the stimuli constituting the problem caused the internal representations of those stimuli to be more substantial.

Although we have discussed the impact of focal consciousness in terms of substantiality, there are other ways to conceptualize its effects. One alternative treats the effect of focal consciousness in terms of *figure* and *ground*. To the extent that a stimulus is processed in focal consciousness, the cognition of that stimulus becomes more figural and less like ground. A second perspective (Taylor & Fiske, 1978) describes the effects of focal consciousness in terms of the concept *salience*. Those authors suggest that focusing on a particular stimulus increases the salience of the cognized stimulus. Another way to interpret the effects of focal consciousness on stimuli processed in that system is in terms of *importance*. To the extent that a stimulus is processed in focal consciousness, it, as represented in consciousness, becomes more important relative to other cognized stimuli.

Regardless of the terminology used, it is clear that processing stimuli in focal consciousness contributes to internal representations of those stimuli. For example, Gelb and Granit (cited in Koffka, 1935) noted that stimuli having the appearance of figure appear to be more solid (i.e., substantial) than stimuli having the appearance of ground. They reasoned that if these perceived differences in the solidity of figure and ground were due to real differences in the internal representations of the stimuli, a figural stimulus (i.e., one processed in focal consciousness to a greater extent) would offer greater resistance to the intrusion of a second stimulus than would a stimulus that had the characteristics of ground (i.e., processed in focal consciousness to a lesser extent). To test this hypothesis, they projected a narrow beam of light onto the figure and the ground of a stimulus configuration. The intensity of the light was increased until it became visible to subjects.

Results indicated that the intensity of the light projected onto the figure had to be greater than that projected onto the ground in order to become visible. This effect strongly implies that increased processing of a stimulus in focal consciousness increases the substantiality of the internal representation of that stimulus.

Similar results have been found in more recent studies. In an experiment carried out by Tesser and Conlee (1975), subjects were asked to rate a series of slides (e.g., a smiling child, a poverty-stricken woman) in terms of their affective reaction to the content of the slides. Subjects were then shown a slide they had previously rated as moderately pleasant or unpleasant and were told to think about how that slide made them feel. There were three experimental variables: (1) whether the slide had originally been rated as pleasant or unpleasant; (2) whether the slide was presented only once or more than once; (3) whether the slide was presented to the subject for 60 seconds or 28 seconds. Subjects then rerated the slide on the pleasant–unpleasant dimension. The results were straightforward. Subjects exposed to the slide for 60 seconds became more extremely positive or negative in their ratings than did subjects exposed to the slide for 28 seconds. Positive versus negative content of the slide and number of presentations did not affect the results. We would interpret these findings in the following way. Assuming a high correlation between the total amount of time that the slides were presented and the amount of time subjects focused on the content of the slides, subjects in the 60-second exposure conditions processed the content of the slides in focal consciousness to a greater extent than did subjects in the 28-second exposure conditions. This increased processing in focal consciousness caused the cognized content of the slides to become more substantial. Because the content of the slides originally evoked an affective reaction, increasing the substantiality of the cognized content increased the intensity of the subjects' affective reactions. This resulted in more extreme ratings of the cognized content of the slides on the pleasant–unpleasant dimension.

McArthur and Solomon (1978) exposed their subjects to individuals who were novel on a physical dimension (e.g., had red hair, wore a leg brace) and thus attracted the focus of attention (cf. Chapter 4) or to individuals who were not novel on any dimen-

FIG. 3.1.

sion. The results of this research indicated that subjects' ratings of the physically novel targets' personality traits (e.g., friendliness and competence) were generally more extreme than were ratings of the nonnovel targets' personality traits. Taylor, Crocker, Fiske, Sprinzen, and Winkler (1979) obtained similar results. Under a wide variety of conditions, subjects rated individuals on whom they focused attention as being friendlier but more nervous than individuals on whom they focused to a lesser degree. This effect also obtains when the target of increased focus is a person's emotional experience. Using a mirror to increase focus on the affective experiences of self, Scheier and Carver (1977) found that subjects in mirror conditions rated their experiences of induced affective states as more extreme than did subjects in no-mirror conditions. Specifically, high self-focus individuals reported being more depressed or elated following exposure to a depression or elation induction manipulation (Velten, 1967) than did low self-focus subjects.

We also find that increased processing in focal consciousness causes the cognized stimulus literally to stand out in consciousness. For example, in Fig. 3.1 the stimulus configuration is constructed so that at any particular point in time the probability of processing the white or the black cross in focal consciousness is approximately equal. As is clearly evident, the cross that is being processed to a greater extent in focal consciousness appears to stand out from its surroundings more than the other cross. Furthermore, the prominence of each cross changes solely as a function of shifts in the extent to which one or the other is processed in focal consciousness.

The results of the research we have reviewed provide fairly strong evidence that the substantiality of internal representations (i.e., cognitions) of stimuli and stimulus events increases as the extent of processing in focal consciousness increases. Because we believe that this dimension of cognition is contributed by focal consciousness, we have referred to it as the dimension of *focalization* (Duval & Hensley, 1976). Variations in the degree to which a cognized stimulus or stimulus event is focalized (i.e., degree of substantiality) are referred to as variations in the degree of focalization. These variations are assumed to be a function of duration x intensity of processing in focal consciousness.

DEGREE OF FOCALIZATION AND ATTRIBUTION

The attributional principle of consistency refers to the degree of similarity among the properties associated with the cognitions of effects and possible causes. We have argued that degree of focalization is a real property associated with any cognized stimulus event that has been processed in focal consciousness. This position suggests that the degree of similarity between cognized events on the dimension of focalization will affect causal attribution. To the extent that a cognized effect (X) is more similar to a cognized possible cause (A) than to other possible causes in terms of degree of focalization, the consistency principle predicts that causality for X will be attributed to A (holding other factors constant). A discussion of research relevant to this hypothesis follows.

In previously published research on the focus of attention and causal attribution, subjects are typically exposed to a situation in which two or more events occur before an effect. The degree of focalization of one of these previously occurring events is increased. This procedure, if done properly, produces conditions in which the degree of focalization of one event is equal to or greater than the degree of focalization of the effect, and the degrees of focalization associated with the remaining events are less than that associated with the effect. Given these circumstances, application of the consistency principle and the second asymmetry criterion to the dimension of focalization predicts that subjects will attribute causality to the event associated with an increased degree of focalization.

Much of the research using this methodology has yielded results that are consistent with the hypothesis. For example, in one of the first studies explicitly concerned with focus of attention and causal attribution, Duval and Wicklund (1973) manipulated the extent to which subjects processed self in focal consciousness. This was accomplished by either exposing or not exposing them to a mirror. Subjects were then asked to imagine themselves in five hypothetical situations. In each situation, a particular effect occurred (e.g., a car accident, a financial windfall). The dependent measure was the extent to which subjects attributed causality for the effects to the actions of self. In this situation, subjects' degrees of focalization in the mirror conditions were presumably equal to or greater than the degree of focalization associated with the effects. The degree of focalization for subjects in the no-mirror conditions was presumably less than the degree of focalization associated with the effects. As predicted by the consistency principle operating within the second asymmetry criterion, subjects in the mirror conditions (i.e., high self-focalization) attributed more causality for the effects to self than did subjects in the no-mirror conditions (i.e., low self-focalization). This general finding has been replicated in other studies (Arkin & Duval, 1975; Storms, 1973).

Similar results have been obtained when the target of the focus of attention is some person or object other than self (Pryor & Kriss, 1977; Regan & Totten, 1975; Taylor & Fiske, 1975). The experiment by Pryor and Kriss (1977) is an excellent example of this research. Based on previous data indicating that people tend to focus more attention on elements that appear earlier in a sentence than on those that appear later, they constructed two sets of statements involving actors, actions, and objects of the actions. In one set of statements, the actor appeared in the sentence before the object of the action (e.g., John laughed at the comedian). Pretest data indicated that this construction caused the actors to be associated with a higher degree of focalization than the objects—a degree of focalization that was presumably equal to or greater than that associated with the actions (e.g., the laughing). In the second set of statements, the object of the action appeared before the actor (e.g., the comedian was laughed at by John). Pretest data indicated that this construction caused the object of the action to be associated with a higher degree of focalization than the actor—again, a degree of focalization that was presumably equal to or greater than that associated with the action. After reading each statement, subjects were asked to attribute some degree of causality for the action (i.e., the effect) to the actor and to the object of the action. As is predicted by our approach, subjects attributed more causality to the element associated with the higher degree of focalization (i.e., the one that appeared first in the sentence).

Although the results of previous research are compatible with predictions derived from applying the consistency principle and the second asymmetry criterion to the dimension of focalization, they do not provide information concerning the validity of all predictions that can be derived from that application. In particular, the consistency principle predicts that people will attribute causality for an effect to the possible cause with a degree of focalization that is most similar to the degree of focalization associated with the effect. For effects that are high, moderate, or low in degree of focalization, subjects should attribute causality to possible causes that are also high, moderate, or low in degree of focalization. A strong test of this prediction requires exposing subjects to an effect that systematically varies in degree of focalization as well as to possible causes that differ in degree of focalization. The following study (Duval & Duval, 1979) attempted to create these conditions.

Subjects were 60 male and female undergraduate students, run in groups ranging in size from 4 to 10. They were first exposed to an effect, a moderately loud piercing sound. The degree of focalization associated with this effect was varied by manipulating the length of time the sound was presented, a method similar to that used by Tesser and Conlee (1975). Subjects either heard the sound for 9 seconds (low-effect focalization conditions), for 15 seconds (moderate-effect focalization conditions), or for 24 seconds (high-effect focalization conditions). All subjects were then told that they would see a videotape showing different people operating three different mechanical devices, one of which had generated the noise they had heard. Their task was to determine which machine had actually caused the sound. In the experimental conditions, the degrees of focalization associated with the three machines and operators were varied by manipulating the total length of time that each machine and operator appeared on the videotape. Specifically,

TABLE 3.1
Frequency of Attribution to Possible Causes

	Effect's Degree of Focalization								
	High			Moderate			Low		
	Machine			Machine			Machine		
	A	B	C	A	B	C	A	B	C
Experimental	0	8	2	2	1	7	6	1	3
Control	4	2	4	5	3	2	3	3	4

subjects in the experimental conditions were shown a video tape that presented machine and operator B for a total of 27 seconds, machine and operator C for a total of 18 seconds, and machine and operator A for a total of 12 seconds. To effect the experimental manipulation as unobtrusively as possible, the videotape of each machine and operator was first cut into 3-second segments. The segments were then spliced together to produce the tape shown to subjects. This tape first presented machine and operator C for 3 seconds, then A for 3 seconds, then C again for 3 seconds, then B for 3 seconds, and so forth. The order of presentation of the 3-second segments was randomly determined but constant for all conditions. This method of presentation was adopted because pretest data indicated that 90% of the subjects exposed to the videotape constructed as described did not spontaneously realize that the machines and operators were presented for different lengths of time. Subjects in control conditions saw a similarly constructed videotape of the three machines and operators. However, in these conditions, each machine and operator was presented for a total of 27 seconds.

After viewing the videotape, subjects were asked to determine which of the three machines and operators had caused the sound. As is clearly evident in Table 3.1, predictions generated by application of the consistency principle and the second asymmetry criterion to the dimension of focalization were supported. In comparison to subjects in control conditions, subjects in the high-effect focalization experimental condition were more likely to attribute causality for the sound to the high-focalization machine and operator B than to the other two possibilities. Subjects in the moderate-effect focalization experimental condition were more likely to attribute causality to the machine and operator that were moderate in level of focalization (i.e., C) than to the machines and operators that were either high or low in degree of focalization. Subjects in the low-effect focalization experimental condition tended to attribute causality to the machine and operator associated with the lowest level of focalization, $\chi^2 (1) = 13.12, p < .001$.

This experiment illustrates how the consistency principle as well as the second asymmetry criterion apply to the dimension of focalization. Given a cognized effect that is associated with a certain degree of focalization, people tend to attribute causality to the possible cause that is most similar to the effect on the dimension of focalization. However, we recognize the limitations of this experiment. The ideal way to test the consistency-focalization hypothesis would be to vary the degree of focalization associated with effects and potential causes without substantially varying factors such as length of presentation or even properties of effects and events that may qualify as possible causes. Until this can be done in a satisfactory manner, results that show the consistency effect on the dimension of focalization will be open to alternative explanation. Furthermore, reliable measurement of the degree of focalization associated with the particular effects and possible causes used in specific experiments will be necessary to fully establish the validity of the proposed relationship between degree of focalization and causal attribution. We do not, however, see the methodological difficulties associated with this area of research as insurmountable and believe that the time and effort spent in developing the necessary methodological innovations will be rewarded by gains in knowledge regarding the relationship between the focus of attention and causal attribution.

In concluding this chapter, we would like to compare our approach with Taylor and Fiske's (1978) treatment of the relationship between the focus of attention and causal attribution. Taylor and Fiske suggest that individuals often attribute causality for some effect to the plausible cause that first comes to mind. The cause that first comes to mind is the cause most available for retrieval from memory. Availability of a cause for retrieval is influenced by the focus of attention. To the extent that a person focuses attention on stimulus *A* rather than *B*, *A* becomes more salient and more available for retrieval from memory. For example, in an actor-observer situation, the observer focuses more attention on the actor than on the actor's external environment. This makes the actor more salient and more available for retrieval from memory than the actor's external environment. When asked to attribute causality for the actor's behavior, the cause that first comes to the observer's mind is the actor. The observer thus attributes causality to the actor (Taylor & Fiske, 1975).

The differences between Taylor and Fiske's (1978) hypothesized role of the focus of attention in the causal-attribution process and our own are clear-cut. Taylor and Fiske would have to predict that increasing focalization or salience of a causal stimulus would increase the tendency to attribute causality to that stimulus. We would predict otherwise, provided that there is more than one previously occurring event present with a degree of focalization equal to or greater than the degree of focalization associated with the effect. Based on the notion of achieving maximum consistency in cause–effect unit formation, our approach predicts that the person would choose a possible cause low in degree of focalization for a low-focalization effect, a possible cause high in degree of focalization for a high-focalization effect, and so forth. In other words, Taylor and Fiske (1978) assume that the focus of attention affects causal attribution in terms of the availability heuristic (Tversky & Kahneman, 1973), whereas we predict that the effect of the focus of attention on causal attribution will conform to the consistency principle.

4 Novelty I

Evidence from Chapter 3 indicates that attribution of causality is influenced by the degree of focalization associated with cognized effects and events that may qualify as possible causes. Data also indicate that the degree of focalization associated with events is directly related to the extent to which attention focuses on those events. This relationship implies that factors affecting the focus of attention will influence the casual-attribution process.

NOVELTY AND THE FOCUS OF ATTENTION

Norman (1976) suggests that the relative *pertinence* of stimuli controls the focus of attention. At any given time, the person is biased to focus on (i.e., to process in focal consciousness) the most pertinent stimulus present in the situation. Most theorists in the area of attention assume that the relative degree of stimulus novelty determines pertinence. To the extent that a stimulus is more novel than other stimuli in the perceptual field, it is more pertinent and will attract the focus of attention. To the extent that a stimulus is less novel, it represents less pertinent information and will be processed in focal consciousness to a lesser extent. We also adopt the general term *novelty* to refer to conditions that determine the extent to which stimuli are processed in focal consciousness.

A review of the extant literature on attention indicates that the concept of novelty is multidimensional. In some cases, novelty is defined in terms of violation of expectation. In others, it is defined in terms of the dynamism of a stimulus (i.e., the extent to which a stimulus changes). Because the literature regarding the relationship between these two dimensions of novelty and the focus of attention is voluminous, we present two selected examples. These are drawn from Sokolov's (Lynn, 1966) research regarding the orienting response because that body of experimental data represents the clearest evidence regarding the relationship between violation of expectation, dynamism, and the focus of attention.

In an experiment designed to investigate the relationship between violation of expectation and the orienting response (i.e., the focus of attention), subjects were first exposed to a 1000 cp tone for 5 seconds. Subjects exhibited a strong orienting response to presentation of this stimulus as measured by various physiological indices (e.g., GSR, heart rate, alpha blocking). Presentation of the 5-second tone was repeated until the person no longer evidenced a general orienting response. On the final trial, the tone was terminated after 3 seconds. Subjects reexhibited an orienting response to this change in stimulus input. We can find no experiment that better illustrates the relationship between violation of expectation and the focus of attention. Subjects had no reason to expect introduction of a tone because they were not told that the experimental procedure involved exposure to sound. Unexpected presentation of a tone thus violated expectation and elicited an orienting response (i.e., attracted the focus of attention). After repeated exposures, the 5-second tone was incorporated into the subject's neuronal model of the situation and, thus, no longer violated expectation. However, termination of the tone after 3 seconds violated expectations derived from this model and elicited an orienting response. Thus, violation of expectation, whether the occurrence of an unexpected event or the nonoccurrence of an expected event, is novel and attracts the focus of attention.

In an experiment designed to investigate the influence of stimulus dynamism on focus of attention, subjects were first exposed and habituated to a 1000 cp tone. During the critical trial, the tone cp was increased from 1000 to 5000. The more rapid the rate of change in tone cp, the greater the magnitude of the orienting response. This seems to be a straightforward demonstration of the effect of stimulus dynamism on the focus of attention. As the stimulus becomes more dynamic (i.e., changes over time), the tendency to focus attention on that stimulus increases.

Quantitative Novelty

In Sokolov's research, novelty is defined in terms of violation of expectation and dynamism. We have proposed (Duval, 1976; Duval & Duval, 1977; Duval & Wicklund, 1972) that the context within which stimuli appear also affects novelty. This proposition is, in part, based on Gestalt principles of field organization, which suggest that stimuli in any perceptual field will be organized in terms of the qualitative similarities and differences between the particular properties of those stimuli. To the extent that individual stimuli have properties that are more similar to each other than to other stimuli in the field and also are proximate to each other, those stimuli will cohere and be perceived as more or less internally homogeneous units or groups (see Koffka, 1935). Each unit or group will be cognitively differentiated from any other unit or group with properties that are qualitatively dissimilar. Furthermore, each unit or group will typically have magnitude (e.g., number, size, amount). Thus, in a simplified perceptual field containing only apples and oranges, the apples and oranges are perceived as two separate groups of stimuli, each with magnitude (e.g., number of stimuli in each group, overall area occupied by each group).

Provided that the stimuli in a particular perceptual field are organized into at least two separate units or groups, we suggest that the novelty of each group will be determined, in part, by the relative magnitude of the two groups. Specifically, to the extent that one group is greater in magnitude than the other on some quantitative dimension(s) shared by both, the lesser of the two groups will be more novel than the greater. Because this dimension of novelty is defined by the quantitative differences between stimuli, we refer to it as *quantitative novelty*.

In order to illustrate the concept of quantitative novelty, let us assume that an individual misreads an invitation to a black-tie cocktail party as an invitation to a costume party. He then arrives at the party in a frog suit. Clearly, a frog in a sea of tuxedos would be novel and attract the focus of attention. Now let us assume that the same person misreads an invitation to a costume party whose theme is frogs as an invitation to a black-tie cocktail party. Consequently, he arrives dressed in a tuxedo but now finds that he is an overdressed newcomer in a field of frogs. Again he would be novel and attract the focus of attention. Finally, let us assume that half of the people invited to a party read the invitation as one to a black-tie cocktail party and the other half interpret it as an invitation to a costume party thematically based on the concept of frogs. Now in this situation, we have half frogs and half in evening dress. The novelty of both is considerably less than when there was only one frog amongst the ties or only one tuxedo amongst the frogs, and attention appears about equally divided between the two groups. But perhaps this effect occurs because the cases in which the person is novel are also cases in which he or she is engaging in inappropriate social behavior. Another example demonstrates that this is not the basis of quantitative novelty.

Let us assume that the perceptual field is limited to a page of words. The words are printed in either italics or roman type and are perceived as two separate groups. In terms of the quantitative-novelty hypothesis, the novelty of either group should depend on the relative number of words in each group. This does, in fact, appear to be the case. When there are few italicized words relative to the number of words in roman type (the usual situation), the italicized words are novel and attract the focus of attention. However, if all but a few of the words on the page are printed in italic type, then the nonitalicized words become novel and attract the focus of attention. Furthermore, if we equalized the number of italicized and nonitalicized words, then neither group would be particularly novel relative to the other and each would clearly be less novel than when either group of words was substantially smaller in number than the other. Inasmuch as other examples (a Russian is novel in America, whereas an American is novel in Russia, etc.) and research (Langer & Imber, 1980; McArthur &

Solomon, 1978) consistently reflect the same relationship between the number in each group and novelty, we conclude that our extension of Gestalt principles to contextual determinants of novelty is essentially correct. Slightly rephrased, to the extent that the properties associated with any stimulus or group of stimuli (A) are infrequently associated with other stimuli in the perceptual field, A will be novel. Further, this relationship should obtain regardless of the particular properties that characterize the different groups of stimuli. That is, in the examples, the novelty of the person's attire, whether frog suit or tuxedo, and the novelty of the features of the type, whether italics or roman, were not determined by some peculiar quality associated with tuxedos, frog suits, italics, or roman type. It was determined by the fact that: (1) the groups were qualitatively different and (2) one group of stimuli was lesser in magnitude than the other. The first point is obvious because novelty cannot exist unless there are differences between stimuli. The second point warrants some additional discussion.

The major point of possible contention between the present view of quantitative novelty and other theories dealing with variables that determine the focus of attention is the following. We have argued that the novelty of a particular group of stimuli is affected by the context in which it appears (i.e., the magnitude of that group relative to the magnitude of proximate but differing groups of stimuli). From this point of view, novelty is situationally determined and in no sense represents an intrinsic quality of the stimulus. Other theorists in this area seem to treat novelty in terms of some property associated with the person (e.g., pregnant, crippled, Black, Chicano) that is intrinsically novel, or they vacillate between treating novelty as intrinsic and as situationally determined. This is not an academic issue. As we see later, quantitative novelty affects causal attribution, and it is essential to realize that the quantitative novelty of effects and events that may qualify as possible causes can change radically from situation to situation as the contexts of those effects and events change.

Although we have discussed the concept of quantitative novelty in terms of a person's attire and type of print, it should be clear that this principle is meant to apply to any property associated with any stimulus. For the sake of simplicity, we accept the general distinction between properties categorized as inherited or innate (e.g., race, sex) and those that reflect the residual effects of the interaction between the stimulus and the world (e.g., memories, personal constructs, facets of a cut diamond). However, we want to draw attention to a type of property that is not clearly subsumed under these two broad categories.

Consider the following case. A person's family, acquaintances, or relatives look to him or her for financial security. The existence of this relationship suggests that a complete description of the person would include the fact that he or she has the property "depended on by others," a property that is just as real as having red hair. Furthermore, this property does not appear to fit into the other two categories. It is certainly not inherited or innate. Nor is it a residual effect of interacting with the world (e.g., memories) because this type of property exists only insofar and to the extent that the relationship between the person and others continues to exist. Thus, we suggest a third group. Properties that fall into this group are produced by the existence of an ongoing relationship between a particular stimulus and other stimuli and will be referred to as *relational properties*.

The concept of relational properties suggests that any type of relationship between two or more people or two or more stimuli necessarily imbues the participants with relational properties. Heider's (1958) classification system suggests that sentiment relationships (e.g., liking for, being liked by) and belonging relation-

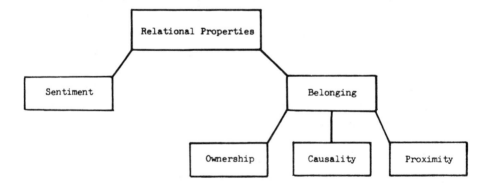

FIG. 4.1   Classification system for relational properties.

ships represent the two major types of relatedness. He further divides the relationship of belonging into three subgroups based on ownership, causality, and proximity (Fig. 4.1). Examples of relationships that we see as falling into each of these groups include the following.

Instances of relationships based on sentiment readily come to mind. If a person feels a certain way toward another (e.g., John loves, hates, or pities Tom), both people have a relational property created and defined by the particular sentiment relationship. The source of the sentiment (John) has the relational property "feels a certain way toward another (Tom)." Likewise, the target of the sentiment (Tom) has the relational property "object of a particular person's feelings." Relational properties based on sentiment can also involve inanimate stimuli. If John likes a film, a painting, a car, etc., these stimuli have the relational property "liked by John." John has the relational property "likes a certain film, painting, car, etc."

The relationship of belonging in the sense of ownership is also easily illustrated. If John owns a blue Ferrari, then he has the relational property "owner of a blue Ferrari." At the same time, the Ferrari has the property "owned by John." Also, instances in which the belonging relationship is created by causality occur frequently. In particular, whenever a person's actions or lack thereof have a particular impact on the world, the causal consequences of the person's behavior or failure to act define a property belonging to that person. For example, if a person's behavior saves lives or causes the destruction of lives, then that person has the relational property "saver of lives" or "destroyer of lives." If a person fails or succeeds at a task, then the failure and success belong to the person by virtue of his or her causal relationship to the outcome. The property that we referred to earlier as "depended on by others" probably falls into this group. Being depended on by others implies that the person's behavior or lack thereof strongly affects the welfare of a particular person or group of people. Similarly, those who are causally affected by a particular person's behavior or lack thereof have the relational property "affected by X."

The same line of thought extends to relationships created by proximity. The property of group membership probably falls into this category. People are known not only by the things that they own or cause but also by membership in particular groups. We say that a person is a Frenchman, a Russian, or a Canadian; that he is a Rotarian, a Catholic, or a Jew—relational properties that result from the greater proximity of a person to one particular group of people than to other groups.

We have proposed that the focus of attention is affected by the quantitative novelty of the properties possessed by any stimulus. These properties can be broken down into three basic groups: inherited or innate, the residual effects of interacting with the world, and relational. Our concept of quantitative novelty and its relationship to the focus of attention predicts that to the extent that any person possesses properties that are infrequently associated with other people, that person will attract the focus of attention. As the extent of processing in focal consciousness increases, the degree of focalization associated with the cognized person will increase. Applying the consistency principle to this situation predicts that causality for some effect will be attributed to the cognized person who is most similar to the effect on the dimension of focalization (provided that the cognized person qualifies as a possible cause for the effect). Thus, given a novel effect (i.e., one that occurs infrequently, violates expectation, is dynamic), attribution of causality should be directed toward a person who is high rather than low in quantitative novelty. In the following section we present data regarding this hypothesis.

Duval and Duval (1977): Experiment 1

To test for the predicted relationship between quantitative novelty, focus of attention, and causal attribution, we gave subjects a description of a novel effect event (i.e., stealing or returning a stolen final examination). Subjects were then given information concerning the characteristics of five people labeled *A*, *B*, *C*, *D*, and *E*, and were told that their task was to determine which of the five individuals might have stolen (returned) the final examination.

In one set of conditions (*D*-similar), the descriptions of the five individuals were equally similar. In a second set of conditions (*D*-dissimilar), person *D*'s description differed from those of the other four which again were equally similar. Thus, in the *D*-similar conditions, person *D* should not have been more quantitatively novel than any other person. In the *D*-dissimilar conditions, person *D* should have been more quantitatively novel than the others because he possessed properties that were occurring infrequently in the relevant social field (i.e., persons *A*, *B*, *C*, and *E*). Accordingly, we predicted that subjects in the *D*-dissimilar conditions would attribute more causality for the novel effect event (stealing or returning the stolen examination) to *D* than would subjects in the *D*-similar conditions.

As a check on the manipulation of the focus of attention, the length of time subjects spent reading the description of *D* was measured. This measurement was important for several reasons. Aside from Pryor and Kriss (1977), who measured focal tendencies in a group of pretest subjects, no study that we are aware of has actually measured the extent to which subjects focus on the various experimental stimuli even though we, as well as others, have claimed that the experimental results of numerous studies have been mediated by the focus of attention. Even though reading time (i.e., looking) is not the ideal measure of the degree of focalization (i.e., intensity as well as duration), it does provide data regarding whether variables are affecting the focus of attention (Berlyne, 1970; Kahneman, 1973).

Subjects were 120 male undergraduate students randomly assigned to one of eight experimental and four control conditions. They were run individually. Each subject was told that the experiment concerned how and why individuals formed impressions of other people when a minimum amount of information concerning those people was available. The experimenter explained that each subject would be given a booklet containing the description of a certain event that had actually taken place on campus. In the experimental conditions, the experimenter added that the booklet also contained descriptions of five people labeled *A*, *B*, *C*, *D*, and

E, who were possibly related to the event. The experimenter then indicated that each subject would be asked to select the person who he thought was causally related to the event in question after reading about the event and characteristics of the five people. Each subject would also be asked to state reasons for his choice.

To establish a base-line reading time for *D*'s description, control groups were included in the design. Instructions given to these subjects were identical to those given to experimental subjects with the following exception. Control subjects were told they would be given the description of one person (rather than five) and asked to determine whether or not (yes–no) this person was causally related to the event in question.

After the initial instructions, the experimenter handed the subjects a booklet containing the experimental material and apparently busied herself with other work during the remainder of the experiment. In actuality, the experimenter positioned herself so that she could measure and record the amount of time subjects spent reading the description of person *D*.

Desirable-Undesirable Event Manipulation

Each subject received a booklet of mimeographed material. The first page described an interaction between a professor and students in his class. Approximately half of the subjects received a booklet indicating that the professor had asked everyone to return their final exam questions. In counting the number of returned exams, however, the professor discovered that one was missing and concluded that it had been stolen (undesirable event condition). The remaining subjects received a booklet that began with the same story about a stolen exam. In this case, however, the story line indicated that some student had anonymously returned the stolen exam with a note saying that he had accidentally found it taped underneath a chair in the classroom where the exam had taken place (desirable event condition). Booklets in all conditions indicated that the professor decided to try to discover who had stolen (returned) the exam in order to punish (reward) that person for being dishonest (honest).

In the experimental conditions, the booklet continued with the following statements:

After looking into the activities and backgrounds of students in his class, the professor eliminated all but five students as possibly related to the incident. The professor gathered information about these students. This information is presented in your booklet. It was obtained from official (e.g., the registrar) and unofficial (e.g., friends and acquaintances) sources. Your task is to read all five descriptions carefully and choose the person A, B, C, D, or E you think stole (returned) the exam. After you have made your choice, please state reasons for that decision.

In the control conditions, this passage was altered where appropriate to state that the subject was dealing with only one person and was to determine whether or not that person stole (returned) the exam.

Target Descriptions

In the experimental conditions, subjects were given five separate sheets describing five people labeled A, B, C, D, and E. Each description specified a person's properties on each of 24 dimensions. In the D-dissimilar conditions, persons A, B, C, and E had similar properties on 16 critical dimensions selected for differentiation. Person D's properties systematically differed from the other four on these dimensions. The content of these properties was counterbalanced. In the Set A conditions, A, B, C, and E had Set A characteristics, whereas D had Set B characteristics. In the Set B conditions, A, B, C, and E had Set B characteristics, whereas D had Set A characteristics. The specific characteristics attributed to each person under Set A and Set B conditions are presented in Table 4.1. In the D-similar conditions, all persons had similar properties on the 16 critical dimensions (i.e., everyone in Set A conditions had properties from Set A; everyone in Set B conditions had Set B properties). In the control conditions, subjects were given one sheet that described person D only. Content of this description was also counterbalanced using the Set A and B characteristics described in Table 4.1.

Each of the five descriptions also included eight noncritical dimensions. On seven of these dimensions, each person had properties that differed from those of the others. All five had a similar property on the remaining dimension (Table 4.2). The particular

TABLE 4.1
Description of 16 Critical Dimensions

Dimension	Set A	Set B
Age	between 18 and 21	between 23 and 25
Weight	between 145 and 152	between 165 and 172
Color of hair	blonde	brown
Scholastic major	humanities	social sciences
Type of residence	rented house	apartment
Pet	cat	dog
Dating habits	frequent dating	occasional dating
Smoking habits	does not smoke	smokes
Gender of siblings	female	male
Location of birthplace	urban area	rural area
Nationality of car	American	foreign
Type of organized social activities	several scholarly activities	several clubs
Number of close friends	many	few
Number of casual acquaintances	few	many
Type of music enjoyed	classical	rock-and-roll
Type of girls preferred	brunette	blonde

TABLE 4.2
Descriptions of Five Persons on Eight Noncritical Dimensions

Dimension	Person A	Person B	Person C	Person D	Person E
Dress	brown coat and tie	blue jeans and sandals	casual shirt and slacks	cut-offs	white Levis and sports shirt
Height	6'	5'10"	5'11"	6'	6'4"
G.P.A.	2.2	2.3	2.6	2.4	2.5
Part-time job	cashier	gardener	clerk in library	Chicken Delight delivery boy	salesman
Drinking habits	light social drinking	light social drinking	light social drinking	light social drinking	light social drinking
Hobbies	bridge	tennis	chess	golf	ping-pong
Type of car	sports car	sedan	sports car	sedan	compact
Alcoholic beverage preferred	dry martini	bourbon on the rocks	whiskey sour	gin and tonic	vodka and tonic

properties attributed to each of the five persons on these eight dimensions were not counterbalanced for content and remained constant over conditions. The order in which the sixteen critical and eight noncritical dimensions appeared in the descriptions was randomly determined but constant across conditions. Thus, properties of each person on the eight noncritical dimensions were randomly mixed in with properties on the sixteen critical dimensions. The primary purpose and effect of randomly mixing the critical and noncritical dimensions in the D-dissimilar conditions (as judged by pretest results) was to minimize experimental demand.

Dependent Measures

After reading the descriptions of the five (one) person(s), each subject indicated which person, A, B, C, D, or E (or D, yes–no), he thought was causally related to the event by writing the person's identifying letter on a piece of paper. Each subject then explained in writing why he had chosen that particular person as causally related to the event. An analysis of these data did not reveal any subject suspicion or knowledge of the experimental hypothesis. In fact, all but one subject constructed logical reasons for their choices based on one or more of the chosen person's described properties. However, one subject in the D-dissimilar condition said that he chose D simply because D was different from the other four. Although this response does not necessarily mean that the subject was aware of the experimental hypothesis, it seemed wisest to eliminate his data from the analysis.

Manipulation Check

To determine whether the experimental manipulation affected subjects' attentional tendencies, the experimenter surreptitiously measured the time each subject spent reading D's description. This measurement was taken using a standard stopwatch calibrated to tenths of a second. To determine if subjects perceived the desirable and undesirable event as differing in morality, each subject was asked to respond to the question "How moral or immoral do you think the event described was?" on a 10-point scale anchored by the appropriate positive and negative labels.

TABLE 4.3
Subjects' Mean Reading Time in Seconds for *D*'s Description

	Desirability of Event					
	Undesirable			*Desirable*		
	D-Dissimilar	*D-Similar*	*Control*	*D-Dissimilar*	*D-Similar*	*Control*
Characteristics Ascribed to D						
Set A	42.6	32.3	30.4	45.3	34.6	33.2
Set B	46.4	35.8	33.1	43.2	28.9	34.9

Results

An analysis of the event-morality question indicated that subjects in the undesirable event conditions perceived the event as more immoral than subjects in the desirable event conditions, $F(1, 112) = 45.67, p < .001$. An analysis of the time of reading data for the experimental conditions revealed a main effect for *D*-dissimilar versus *D*-similar. Subjects in the *D*-dissimilar conditions took longer to read *D*'s description than subjects in the *D*-similar conditions, $F(1, 112) = 8.56, p < .01$ (means presented in Table 4.3). No other reliable main effects or interactions were found. To establish the direction of this difference, an analysis was performed on time of reading data from the *D*-similar and the control conditions. This analysis did not reveal the presence of any main effects or interactions between these two conditions. This suggests that the longer time for reading *D*'s description in the *D*-dissimilar conditions was due to an increase in time of reading in those conditions rather than a decrease in the *D*-similar conditions. Thus, the quantitative novelty manipulation apparently affected subjects' foci of attention in the expected manner.

The primary experimental hypothesis suggested that person *D* would be chosen by subjects as the cause of the effect (i.e., stolen exam, returned exam) more frequently when *D* differed from the other four stimulus persons. Fifty-seven percent of the subjects in the *D*-dissimilar conditions chose person *D* as causally related to the effect. Fifteen percent of the subjects in the *D*-similar conditions chose *D* as causally related to the effect (Table 4.4). The difference between these proportions is reliable, $\chi^2 (1) = 15.62, p < .01$. In addition, there was no effect for the desirable versus undesirable event, $\chi^2 < 1$, no effect for Set A versus Set B characteristics, $\chi^2 < 1$ and no interaction between level of similarity and desirability of the event or level of similarity and sets of characteristics, $z < 1$ in all cases.

Experiment 2

In experiment 1, subjects chose person D as causally related to the effect more often when D was quantitatively novel. By implication, the magnitude of the *qualitative* differences between D and others should also affect the novelty of D, the focus of attention, and attribution of causality. For example, if shape is the dimension on which two groups of elements differ, a small group of triangles would be more novel than an equally small group of ovals relative to a larger group of circles. Thus, the greater the qualitative differences between larger and smaller groups, the greater the novelty of the smaller group; the greater the novelty of a group of elements, the greater the tendency for attention to focus on that group. This generates a second hypothesis concerning novelty and causal attribution: holding the quantitative magnitude of two differing groups constant, the greater the magnitude of qualitative differences between the smaller and larger group, the greater the tendency to attribute causality for a novel effect to the smaller group.

An experiment was designed to test this hypothesis. Subjects were 77 female undergraduate students. They were run in groups ranging in size from 15 to 20. Each subject was randomly assigned to one of eight conditions. This experiment followed the same procedure as experiment 1 with the following exceptions. Although the characteristics used to describe the five students were the same as in the first experiment, approximately half the subjects received a booklet containing descriptions of five individuals labeled A, B, C, D, and E in which person D was systematically different from A, B, C, and E on only five of the sixteen dimensions used in the earlier experiment to differentiate D from the other four persons (low novelty condition). Persons A, B, C, and E were similar to

TABLE 4.4
Number of Subjects Who Chose or Did Not Choose Person D

Set of Characteristics Ascribed to Person D	Undesirable Event				Desirable Event				Total	
	D-Dissimilar		D-Similar		D-Dissimilar		D-Similar			
	Chose D	Chose Not D	Chose D	Chose Not D	Chose D	Chose Not D	Chose D	Chose Not D	Chose D	Chose Not D
Set A	4	6	2	8	7	3	1	9	14	26
Set B	6	4	1	9	6	4	2	8	15	25
Total	10	10	3	17	13	7	3	17		

each other on all 16 dimensions. The remaining subjects received a booklet containing descriptions of five individuals in which person D was systematically different from A, B, C, and E on all sixteen crucial dimensions (high novelty condition); A, B, C, and E were similar on these dimensions. The sets of characteristics, A and B, were counterbalanced as in the previous experiment, and the variable of desirable–undesirable event was included. The dependent measure was the choice of person as causally related to the event. After making their choices, subjects were asked to indicate reasons for their selection. Again, no subject indicated that her choice was related to awareness of the experimental hypothesis. However, two subjects in the high novelty condition did indicate that they had chosen D simply because he differed from the others. Again, this does not mean that these choices were in response to any perceived experimental demand. However, in accordance with the earlier criterion, the data from these subjects were dropped from the analysis.

Results

The experimental hypothesis suggested that subjects would choose person D as causally related to the event more frequently in the high novelty than in the low novelty conditions and that this tendency would operate independently of the desirability of the event. The obtained data indicated that 75% of the subjects in high novelty conditions chose person D as causally related to the event in question, whereas 22% of the subjects in the low novelty conditions chose person D as the cause of the event. This difference is reliable by chi-square, χ^2 (1) = 6.70, p < .01. No differences were found for the variable of event desirability, χ^2 = 1.64, for Set A versus Set B, $\chi^2 < 1$, or for interactions between any of the three independent variables, $z < 1$ in all cases.

Experiment 3

If the high and low novel persons of experiment 2 were included in the same social aggregate, this formulation would make the same prediction. Subjects should tend to choose the high novel person as the cause of a novel effect more frequently than the low novel person. This prediction is based on the following reasoning. Even though both persons would be novel relative to the surrounding group (A, B, C, and E), to the extent that the high novel person differs from this group on more dimensions than does the low novel person, the former should attract the focus of attention and causal attribution (given moderate to high effect novelty). Thus, we have the following hypothesis. In a social aggregate: (1) made up of individuals who could have caused an event and (2) organized into three distinct areas of the perceptual field on the basis of similarities and dissimilarities, causality for a novel effect will be attributed to the most qualitatively novel stimulus (i.e., person). The desirability of the effect to be explained should not affect this outcome.

An experiment was designed to test this hypothesis. Subjects were 92 male undergraduates. They were run in groups ranging in size from 15 to 20. Each subject was randomly assigned to one of sixteen conditions. Experiment 3 used the same procedures as experiment 2 with the following exceptions. In the C and E novel conditions, subjects were given descriptions of six people. Four were described as similar on the sixteen critical dimensions, one was described as differing from the others on five of the sixteen dimensions, and one was described as differing from the others on all sixteen critical dimensions. In the nonnovel conditions, all six persons were described as similar on the sixteen critical dimensions. The design was counterbalanced for content of description as in experiments 1 and 2 and included the variable of desirable–undesirable event. The order in which the two dissimilar persons were presented was counterbalanced in the following way. Approximately one half of the subjects were given booklets containing descriptions of six people in which person C was the low novel person and E the high novel person. The remaining subjects were given booklets in which the order of presentation of the high and low novel person was reversed. However, for purposes of clarity, we refer to the high novel person as E and the low novel person as C. The dependent measure was the subject's choice of A, B, C, D, E, or F as the cause of the described effect. After subjects had made their selections, they were asked to write down their reasons for making the choice. No subjects indicated any suspicion concerning the purposes of the experiment or that they had chosen the person simply because he was different.

Results

Experiment 3 was designed to measure the tendency to attribute causality in a situation where there is more than one quantitatively novel person and the two or more novel people differ with regard to degree of qualitative novelty. The experimental hypothesis suggested that subjects in the C and E novel conditions would tend to choose the high novel person (E) more frequently than the low novel person (C). Thus, we are primarily interested in a comparison of the frequency with which subjects in the C and E novel and nonnovel conditions chose C and E as the cause of the effect.

By partitioning the chi-square contingency table (Bresnahan & Shapiro, 1966), it is possible to isolate and compare the frequency with which subjects in the C and E novel conditions versus those in the nonnovel conditions chose persons C and E as the cause of the effect. The chi-square analysis of the partitioned table indicates that, in comparison to the proportion of subjects who attributed causality to persons C and E in the nonnovel conditions, a greater proportion of subjects in the C and E novel conditions chose the high novel person (E) as the cause of the effect rather than the low novel person, $\chi^2 (1) = 5.33$, $p < .05$. This result is consistent with the experimental hypothesis. In addition, no effect was found for content of descriptions, $\chi^2 < 1$, desirability of the effect, $\chi^2 < 1$, or order of presentation, $\chi^2 < 1$. On inspection, the pattern of obtained data does not seem to indicate the presence of any interactive effects involving the four independent variables.

We have seen that events that: (1) violate expectations; (2) are dynamic; or (3) are quantitatively novel attract the focus of attention. We propose that the relationship between violation of expectation and focus of attention, coupled with the relationship between the focus of attention and causal attribution offers an alternative way to interpret some of the data now explained in terms of correspondent inference theory (Jones & Davis, 1965). The relationship between quantitative novelty, the focus of attention, and causal attribution mediates consensus, distinctiveness, and salience effects.

CORRESPONDENT INFERENCE

Correspondent inference theory argues that a person's behavior conveys maximum information about actual attitudes and beliefs when the person has freely chosen to engage in a behavior that has a low prior probability of occurrence. For example, in research conducted by Jones and Harris (1967), subjects read a speech supposedly written by a debate student. This speech either argued that Castro's Cuba was a legitimate nation (pro-Castro conditions) or that it was not (anti-Castro conditions). Subjects were told either that the student chose to present the pro-Castro position or that the position had been assigned. It was assumed that the prior probability of a student taking a pro-Castro stand of his or her own free will would be lower than the prior probability of a student advocating a pro-Castro position because it had been assigned. Under these circumstances, correspondent inference theory predicts more attribution of responsibility for the content of the essay to the author's true feelings in the former case. This prediction was supported. Subjects in the pro-Castro-choice condition believed that the author of the speech had stronger pro-Castro feelings than did subjects in the pro-Castro-no choice condition.

From the present point of view, the correspondent inference effect reflects the relationship between violation of expectation, focus of attention, and causal attribution. For example, in Jones and Harris (1967), subjects probably assumed that students given a choice between arguing for or against Castro would not pick the pro-Castro position just as subjects in Sokolov's violation of expectation experiment did not expect to hear a tone. When the debater freely chose to present a pro-Castro position, he violated subjects' expectations just as presentation of the tone in Sokolov's experiment violated expectations. Because an event that violates expectation attracts the focus of attention, the debater who freely chose to advocate the pro-Castro position presumably attracted subjects' foci of attention and was thus associated with a high degree of focalization. In the pro-Castro-no choice condition, the debater's behavior would violate subjects' expectations to a lesser extent because the debater was simply responding to a legitimate request. Thus, the debater in that condition would be associated with a lesser degree of focalization than the debater in the pro-Castro-choice condition. Now if we assume that the effect, the content of the essay, was also associated with a fairly high degree of focalization because it was quantitatively novel (i.e., occurred infrequently), application of the consistency principle and the second asymmetry criterion to the dimension of focalization predicts a stronger tendency to attribute causality for the effect to the debater in the pro-Castro-choice conditions than in the pro-Castro-no choice conditions, a prediction that is entirely consistent with the results obtained in those conditions.

The same analysis can be applied to the astronaut-submariner study (Jones, Davis, & Gergen, 1961). When the job applicant told the prospective employer that his personality fit the job description, he was engaging in expected behavior. When the applicant described his personality in terms that were diametrically opposed to those listed as optimally desirable for the job, he violated expectation. Consequently, subjects attributed more causality for the effect (i.e., the applicant's description of self) to internal properties of the person when he violated expectation.

QUANTITATIVE NOVELTY, CONSENSUS, DISTINCTIVENESS, AND SALIENCE

The obtained relationship between quantitative novelty, focus of attention, and causal attribution (Duval & Duval, 1977) generalizes the concepts of consensus and distinctiveness (Kelley, 1967, 1971, 1973). For example, in the typical manipulation of consensus (McArthur, 1972), subjects are told that someone (e.g., John) has properties that either occur infrequently (low consensus) or frequently (high consensus). More specifically, low-consensus information indicates that John likes something, does something, etc., but few others like the item, do that particular thing, etc. High-consensus information indicates that almost everyone else shares John's attitude, engages in the same behavior, and so forth. In low-consensus information conditions, subjects usually attribute more causality to John for his attitude, behavior, etc., than in high-consensus information conditions. From the present point of view, the consensus manipulation is a manipulation of the person's level of quantitative novelty, and the attribution effect is due to the relationship between quantitative novelty, the focus of attention, and causal attribution. To the extent that a person has properties that occur infrequently (low consensus), that person is quantitatively novel and attracts the focus of attention and causal attribution. To the extent that a person has properties also characteristic of other people (high consensus), that person is low in quantitative novelty and does not attract the focus of attention or attribution of causality.

The relationship between distinctiveness and causal attribution yields to a similar analysis. For example, when John likes a comedian, the comedian possesses the relational property "liked by John." To the extent that John does not like other comedians (high distinctiveness manipulation), the comedian has a relational property "liked by John," which occurs infrequently in the population of comedians. Thus, by definition, the comedian is quantitatively novel and attracts the focus of attention and causal attribution. Of course, the converse is also true. To the extent that John likes all comedians (low distinctiveness manipulation), the comedian's relational property "liked by John" occurs frequently in the population of comedians. The comedian is thus low in quantitative novelty and receives less attribution of causality for John's reaction to him.

The concept of quantitative novelty and its relationship to causal attribution also applies to research concerning the effects of salience on the attribution process. For example, McArthur and Solomon (1978) showed subjects a videotape of a discussion between two women concerning the outcome of a bridge game. During the course of the discussion, one person (the aggressor) became highly critical of the other person's (the victim's) performance. The salience of the victim was varied in terms of her physical appearance. In one set of conditions, she either did (high salience) or did not (low salience) have red hair. In a second set of conditions, she was shown either wearing (high salience) or not wearing (low salience) a leg brace. The results of the experiment indicated that subjects attributed more causality for the aggressor's behavior to the victim when she was salient than when she was not. We interpret this effect as reflecting the influence of quantitative novelty on causal attribution. The property of having red hair or wearing a leg brace occurs infrequently in the general population. People who have these properties are thus quantitatively novel, attract the focus of attention, and, as in McArthur and Solomon's study, receive a disproportionate share of causality for their contribution to an effect event.

ACTORS AND QUANTITATIVE NOVELTY

There is an additional point to be addressed. Hansen and Donoghue (1977) claim that actors are affected by quantitative novelty information to a lesser degree than observers even when given the type of assurances used by Wells and Harvey (1977) regarding the representativeness of the information. Except for the fact that actors tend to believe that other people will behave, think, etc., as they do (Ross, Greene, & House, 1977) and thus do not view themselves as quantitatively novel, we can find no legitimate reason for thinking that actors should be immune to quantitative novelty information concerning themselves. Because this is an important point, we present evidence that actors who are led to believe that they are quantitatively novel do tend to increase in level of self-focus (Duval & Siegel, 1978).

Subjects were 43 male undergraduates. They were randomly assigned to four experimental conditions and run individually. After the subject was seated, the experimenter explained that the experiment concerned personality and judgment but that a separate item of business had to be taken care of before the actual experiment could begin. The subject was told that Dr. Robertson of the psychology department had been developing a psychological testing instrument using information taken from the questionnaires filled out at the beginning of the semester by students in introductory psychology classes. He was told that the psychology department had a rule stating that faculty using information about students must inform the students about the nature of the information in their possession. Dr. Robertson had asked graduate students running experiments to help him fulfill this obligation.

The experimenter then handed the subject an envelope with his name on it, indicating that students at various schools had filled out the same attitude questionnaire and that Dr. Robertson had taken what he believed to be a person's 10 most important attitudes from this questionnaire. The subject was told that Dr. Robertson determined for each individual, the extent to which others in the total sample of about 10,000 people from various colleges and universities held similar or different positions on each of the attitude dimensions. The experimenter indicated that the information in the envelope contained no reference to any particular attitude because Dr. Robertson was only interested in a person's 10 most important attitudes and the extent to which each individual in the sample held the same or different attitudes as others. The experimenter continued by indicating that upon opening the envelope the subject would find 11 cards with circles drawn on them and that part of each circle would be darkened. The darkened part supposedly represented the proportion of the total sample of 10,000 people who held the same attitude as the subject. The experimenter then said that the information was strictly confidential, known only to Dr. Robertson, and that he was supposed to wait outside while the subject looked at it. When he returned, he told the subject to keep the envelope because he was the only person who was to have access to the information.

In reality each subject was given an envelope containing one of two sets of cards. In the low-agreement conditions, subjects were given 10 randomly arranged cards with circles having from 1% to 10% of the total area darkened. The darkened area on the 11th summary card was equal to 5% of the total area of the circle. In the high-agreement conditions, subjects were given 10 cards with circles having from 90% to 99% of the total area darkened. The summary card's circle was 95% dark.

After the subject had ample time to examine the cards, the experimenter reentered the cubicle and told the subject that he was to participate in a study concerning the relationship between personality and various types of judgmental processes. The experimenter then asked the subject to respond to a brief personality inventory. The experimenter explained that the personality test was the Lusher Color-Word Inventory, a measure designed to study personality as a function of color sensitivity. Subjects were told that the test involved seeing a series of cards, each of which would have a different word printed on it. Each word would also be printed in a particular color. The subject's task was to name the color of each word as soon as he perceived it.

Following these instructions, subjects were presented with five words that were either self-relevant (self-relevant word conditions) or nonself-relevant (nonself-relevant word conditions) in content. The self-relevant words were *me, myself, I, self,* and *face.* The nonself relevant words, matched for frequency of usage, length, and number of syllables were *up, theory, a, week,* and *tool.* Each word was printed on an individual sheet of white poster paper measuring 30 x 50 cm. Colors were randomly assigned to words. Each word was presented separately, and the order of presentation was random. The dependent measure was latency of response to the color-naming task. Latency was measured by a concealed experimental aide.

The experimental hypothesis predicted that self-focus would be elevated for subjects in the low agreement conditions. According to Geller and Shaver (1976), any increase in self-focus is reflected in longer color-naming latencies for self-relevant words relative to nonself-relevant words. Thus, we expected color-naming latencies to be longer in the low agreement-self-relevant word condition than in any other condition. An analysis of mean color-naming latencies revealed the predicted interaction between quantitative novelty and type of word, $F(1, 39) = 8.23, p < .01$. As inspection of Table 4.5 indicates, subjects in the low agreement-self-relevant word condition evidenced longer color-naming latencies than subjects in any other condition. Thus, it would appear that the frequency with which a property of self occurs in a social aggregate

TABLE 4.5
Mean Latency of Color-Naming Response in Seconds

	5%	*95%*
Self-Relevant	5.4	1.2
Nonself-Relevant	1.5	1.4

Note: As means increase, latency of color-naming response increases.

does affect a person's level of quantitative novelty and tendency to focus on self. These results clearly indicate that an actor's focus of attention is affected by information concerning his level of quantitative novelty. In view of this rather unequivocal evidence, we must conclude that the effect of quantitative novelty on focus of attention does not vary as a function of the role of the person (i.e., actor versus observer) provided that the various factors affecting the impact of such information are taken into account (Kassin, 1979; Kulik & Taylor, 1980).

SUBJECTIVE FREQUENCY ESTIMATES AND ATTRIBUTION

With the exception of McArthur and Solomon (1978), we have discussed research in which the quantitative novelty of a possible cause was explicitly and effectively manipulated. In the absence of an effective manipulation, it is clear that the individual's subjective estimates of the frequency with which properties occur will determine who or what is seen as quantitatively novel (Kassin, 1979; Nisbett & Borgida, 1975; Wells & Harvey, 1977). For example, McArthur and Post (1977) exposed subjects to four people. One was wearing a red shirt, and the other three were wearing identical green shirts. McArthur and Post (1977) predicted that subjects would attribute more causality to the red-shirted person because he was clearly quantitatively novel in that situation. We would have made the same prediction given that quantitative novelty was defined entirely by the experimental situation. In fact, the opposite results were obtained. Subjects attributed more causality to the three people wearing green shirts than to the supposedly novel person wearing the red shirt. In analyzing this outcome, it became clear that McArthur and Post (1977) may have overlooked the possibility that subjects' personal estimates concerning frequency of occurrence rather than the explicit experimental manipulation determined quantitative novelty, focus of attention, and causal attribution in this situation. Specifically, subjects may have seen the group of three people wearing identical shirts as the more novel stimulus because they estimated that this class of stimuli occurs infrequently. In fact, aside from some occupations (e.g., sports), we cannot think of many instances in which one would encounter three people wearing identical dress. Thus, the unexpected results found by McArthur and Post (1977) may have been due to the tendency for subjective estimates concerning frequency of occurrence to take precedence over an explicit but weaker manipulation of that variable.

The impact of the false consensus bias on causal attribution (Ross, Greene, & House, 1977) further illustrates this point. Subjects were first asked to wear a sandwich sign while walking about the campus. Some subjects agreed to this request and others refused. Subjects were then asked to estimate what proportion of their peers would make the same choice that they had made. Both groups of subjects (agreed or refused) indicated that a majority of their peers would make the same decision (i.e., subjects evidenced the false consensus bias in estimating population characteristics). After obtaining these data, subjects made judgments about the personality of a person who supposedly had made the same or a different decision than they. The results indicated that subjects made more confident and extreme inferences about the personality traits of the differing other than the similar other, implying that they attributed more causality for the differing other's choice to internal dispositional qualities (Kassin, 1979). This finding strikes us as a clear quantitative novelty effect (although violation of expectation may also be involved). Subjects believed, for whatever reason, that their choice reflected a behavioral property that was common to a majority (approximately 60% to 70%) of the relevant population. A person who behaved differently had, from the subjects' point of view, an infrequently occurring behavioral property. Properties that occur infrequently are quantitatively novel and attract the focus of attention and causal attribution. Thus, in the absence of a manipulation that alters subjects' frequency estimates, using the principle of quantitative novelty in causal attribution research requires that the predictor know the person's subjective notions concerning what does and does not occur frequently.

In summary, we have proposed that the focus of attention is

determined by novelty. We have discussed three types of novelty—violation of expectation, dynamism, and quantitative novelty. We have cited evidence indicating that a substantial amount of attributional research can be interpreted in terms of the effect of two of these types of novelty on the focus of attention and causal attribution. Violation of expectation generalizes the correspondent inference effect. Quantitative novelty integrates previously unrelated variables such as distinctiveness, consensus, and stimulus salience. Although available evidence is inconclusive, dynamism, the third type of novelty, appears to mediate or plays a highly significant role in mediating the fundamental attribution error (Ross, 1977). In the following chapter, we present an additional variation on the concept of quantitative novelty.

5 Novelty II

In the previous chapter, quantitative novelty was discussed in terms of the frequency of occurrence. To the extent that a person possesses a property that is infrequently possessed by other people, he or she is quantitatively novel and attracts the focus of attention and causal attribution. However, frequency of occurrence is only one aspect of the principle that forms the basis of the general concept of quantitative novelty—the relationship *greater than/lesser than*. That is to say, a property that occurs infrequently is novel because the number of people who have that property is less than the number of people who do not have that property or have a different property. Thus, the phrase "frequency of occurrence of a property" is just one way to express the fact that the magnitude of one property (*A*), as measured in terms of number of people who have that property, is greater or lesser than the magnitude of a differing property (*B*), also measured in terms of the number of people who have that property. In this chapter, we discuss the concept of quantitative novelty in terms of the relative magnitude or amount of the various properties that people possess.

While people have properties that occur with greater or lesser frequency in the population, it is also clear that many of these properties have magnitude in and of themselves. For example, while intelligence is an infrequently occurring property in the world and makes people novel relative to plants, the magnitude of intelligence itself can vary. John may have more or less intelligence than Mary. Strictly speaking, the person with less of the property than the other constitutes a smaller area of the field (provided that the two people and that dimension make up the entire field). Because the general greater than/lesser than relationship defines quantitative novelty, the person with the smaller amount of the property (in this case, intelligence) should be quantitatively novel on that dimension and attract the focus of attention. Differences in physical size are an interesting case in point. Standing next to Wilt Chamberlain, a person of average height definitely feels like he or she is the lesser of the two and has a pronounced tendency to focus on self. Conversely, standing next to a 3-foot-tall child, one sees the child as the lesser and tends to focus attention on him or her. Differences in power and prestige offer an equally interesting example. An average individual who meets the President of the United States experiences self as a small part of the world compared to the Presidency and clearly focuses attention on self. But encountering the young boy who delivers interdepartmental mail produces the opposite effect. He is the smaller area of the field with regard to power and prestige, and attention definitely is focused on the other rather than self.

The frequency-of-occurrence type of quantitative novelty and the magnitude form of the concept can be independent of one another and thus do not always operate in the same direction. For instance, a millionaire would be low in quantitative novelty with regard to magnitude of wealth because he or she possesses more money, land, etc., than most other people. However, the property "being a millionaire," occurs infrequently in the general population. In terms of frequency of occurrence, then, the millionaire would be high in quantitative novelty. In these cases, we assume that the dimension of quantitative novelty that controls the focus of attention is situationally determined.

The plausibility of the magnitude form of quantitative novelty is admittedly not as intuitive as the frequency-of-occurrence aspect of the concept. Nevertheless, it follows directly from the basic principle from which the concept of quantitative novelty is derived. To provide evidence regarding this notion, Duval and Siegel (1978)

manipulated quantitative novelty with regard to one of four properties: wealth, prestige, power, or physical prowess. This
manipulation was accomplished by asking subjects to become
(i.e., role play) a person who had either a large or small amount of
one of the properties. (Although role playing as an experimental
technique has its pros and cons, the reader is referred to articles by
Bem, 1965, Geller, 1978, Holmes & Bennett, 1974, Kruglanski,
1975, and Willis & Willis, 1970, for research supporting the use of
role-playing techniques in the context of this particular study.) In
this experiment, the predicted tendency for the magnitude type of
quantitative novelty to affect the focus of attention was tested by
measuring the subject's tendency to focus on self. This measurement was obtained by giving subjects a modified version of the
Stroop Color-Word Test (Geller & Shaver, 1976), designed to
measure degree of self-focus (see Chapter 4). It was predicted that
subjects who played the role of a person having a relatively small
amount of any one of the four properties would evidence higher
levels of self-focus than subjects who played the role of a person
having a relatively large amount of the same property.

Sixty-eight female undergraduates volunteered to participate in
the experiment, were randomly assigned to one of sixteen experimental conditions, and were run individually. They were
ushered into an experimental cubicle constructed so that a concealed
confederate could monitor the subject's behavior during the experiment.

The experimenter began by explaining that the study concerned
the extent to which people were able to role play different
roles—the degree to which different individuals could "get into
another person's skin." Subjects were told that they would be
given a brief description of another person and would be asked to
become this person during the experiment. Subjects were en-
couraged to role play naturally and to feel as little embarrassment
or shyness as possible. At this point, the experimenter handed subjects a written description of the person they were to role play and
left the laboratory.

After a brief time interval, the experimenter reentered the
laboratory and confirmed that the subject understood exactly
what the task involved. To facilitate the subject's transition into

the role, the experimenter asked each to respond to three items as though they were the person described. These items were: "Tell me something about yourself"; "What is your life like?"; and "How do you feel about yourself?". The length of subjects' responses to these questions ranged from 4 to 6 minutes.

At this point, the experimenter asked the subject to respond to a brief personality inventory. The experimenter explained that the personality test was the Lusher Color-Word Inventory, a measure designed to study personality as a function of color sensitivity. Subjects were told that this test was included in the experiment to determine the extent to which role playing a particular person would be reflected in an actual measure of personality. Subjects were told that the test involved seeing a series of cards, each of which would have a different word printed on it in a particular color. The subject's task was to name the color of each word as rapidly as possible. Subjects were then reminded to remain in the role they had assumed while responding to this test.

Following these instructions, subjects were presented with five words that were either self-relevant (self-relevant word conditions) or nonself-relevant (nonself-relevant word conditions) in meaning. Each word was presented separately, and the order of presentation was random. The dependent measure was latency of response on the color-naming task. Latency was measured by the concealed confederate using a stopwatch calibrated to tenths of a second.

Each role description asked subjects to become a person who had a relatively large amount (high conditions) or small amount (low conditions) of one of four different properties: wealth, prestige, power, or physical prowess. For example, the high-wealth role asked subjects to become a person who had a yearly income and total financial assets exceeding $100,000. The low-wealth role asked subjects to become a person whose yearly income was $6,000 with total assets of less than $500. The high–low role descriptions regarding the other three properties followed the same pattern. Subjects were asked to become a person known and respected by many other persons (high prestige), a person who had a great deal of control over the lives of other persons (high power), or a person who possessed substantial abilities to do various motor tasks (high physical prowess). In the low conditions, subjects were asked to become a person who was not known or respected by others (low prestige), a person who had little control over the lives of others (low power), or a person who had little ability to do motor tasks (low physical prowess).

Using a slightly modified version of the Geller and Shaver (1976) procedure, five self-relevant and five nonself-relevant words were printed on individual sheets of white poster board measuring 30 × 50 cm. The self-relevant words were *me, myself, I, self*, and *face*. The nonself-relevant words, matched with the self-relevant set for frequency of usage, length, and number of syllables, were *up, theory, a, week*, and *tool*. Colors were randomly assigned to words.

The mean latency of color-naming response time was computed for each subject. An analysis of these data (Table 5.1) revealed significant main effects for type of word, $F(1, 52) = 7.82, p < .01$, and high-low quantitative position, $F(1, 52) = 9.83, p < .01$. However, these main effects were qualified by the predicted type of word × quantitative position interaction, $F(1, 52) = 6.81, p < .05$. Inspection of this interaction pattern indicates that, as predicted, subjects in the low self-relevant word conditions generally evidenced longer color-naming latencies than subjects in any other condition. No differences between the high self-relevant word, low nonself-relevant word, or high nonself-relevant word conditions were observed. Nor were any other main effects or interactions found.

An analysis of simple effects indicated that the type of word × quantitative position interaction was significant for the power, prestige, and physical prowess conditions. Although in the right direction, the predicted interaction in the wealth conditions was not significant. Instead, the analysis revealed a main effect for type of word, $F(1, 52) = 5.32, p < .05$. Further analysis of this latter effect indicated that subjects in both the low and high wealth conditions took longer to name the color of self-relevant words than the color of nonself-relevant words. In addition, there were no differences in color-naming latency between the high and low wealth self-relevant word conditions.

Results from this experiment indicate that subjects associated with a small amount of any one of the four properties were generally more self-focused (as measured by our version of the Stroop Color-Word Test) than subjects associated with a larger

TABLE 5.1
Subjects' Mean Latency of Response Time (in Seconds)
to Color-Naming Task

Quantitative Position		Wealth		Power		Prestige		Physical Prowess	
		Low	High	Low	High	Low	High	Low	High
Self-Relevant Word	n	4	4	4	5	6	4	5	4
	M	2.46	2.19	1.86	1.31	4.06	1.40	7.92	1.40
Nonself-Relevant Word	n	4	4	4	5	4	4	4	5
	M	1.32	1.41	1.32	1.14	1.37	1.37	1.48	.98

Note: As means increase, latency of color-naming response increases.

amount of those same properties. These findings are consistent with the quantitative novelty-focus of attention hypothesis. The quantitative novelty of a person's self can be defined in terms of the relative magnitude of properties associated with self and functions as a determinant of attention. In addition, we assume that the obtained relationship between a person's quantitative novelty (defined in terms of magnitude) and the tendency to focus on self is the same relationship that exists between a person's degree of this form of quantitative novelty and the tendency for others to focus on that person. That is to say, to the extent that a person possesses properties that are lesser in magnitude than properties possessed by others in the social field, all persons should tend to focus on the quantitatively novel person. Further, although we did not measure causal attribution in this study, we assume that the relationship between focus of attention and causal attribution specified by the consistency principle and found in previously mentioned studies still holds when the focus of attention is determined by the magnitude rather than by the frequency form of quantitative novelty.

Of the four properties used in this study, the predicted interaction was found for all properties but wealth. In the wealth conditions, subjects who role played a person high in wealth were as self-focused as subjects who played the low-wealth role. A survey conducted after these results were obtained may explain this deviation from prediction. A sample of 150 subjects indicated that persons who made $100,000 per year, the major property of the high-wealth role, were seen as comprising a very small proportion of the population, $M = 3\%$. This finding suggests that subjects who role played the high-wealth role also believed that the type of person they had become (i.e., were role playing) occurred infrequently in the general population. This would mean that subjects in the high-wealth role were *low* in quantitative novelty in terms of magnitude but *high* in quantitative novelty in terms of frequency of occurrence. Depending on the way in which each aspect of quantitative novelty contributes to overall novelty, this situation could have caused subjects in the high-wealth condition to be as novel or almost as novel as subjects in the low-wealth condition. This, in turn, could explain why subjects in the high-wealth condition were as self-focused as subjects in the low-wealth condition. Overall, both groups were approximately equal with regard to the combined forms of quantitative novelty. This possibility emphasizes the need to understand more clearly how the different forms of quantitative novelty interact to define the overall novelty of a property and, thus, the tendency to focus on and attribute causality to the person associated with that property. We should also include the contributions of dynamism and violation of expectation to overall novelty in this problem.

Alternative Explanations

Although the experimental results are entirely compatible with the quantitative novelty-focus of attention hypothesis, other possible explanations for the effects should be considered. For example, because subjects apparently assumed their respective roles in a psychologically meaningful manner, one might argue that subjects in the low conditions experienced greater anxiety than subjects in the high conditions. Presumably this would occur because having a small amount of any of the four properties is not as socially desirable as having a large amount and might be associated with hardship, low status, etc. As the Stroop Color-Word Test is a complex task (Glass & Singer, 1972) and high levels of anxiety decrease performance on complex tasks (Spence & Spence, 1966), any anxiety induced by the low roles would decrease performance on this test. However, this reasoning predicts decreased performance in both the low self-relevant word and low nonself-relevant word conditions. Inasmuch as this effect did not occur, the efficacy of an anxiety interpretation of the obtained results requires some factor that would produce anxiety in the low self-relevant word conditions but not in the low nonself-relevant word conditions.

One possibility involves the difference between the types of words to which subjects in each condition were exposed. For example, exposing subjects who had adopted undesirable roles to self-relevant as opposed to nonself-relevant words may have augmented their levels of anxiety. If this occurred, subjects in the low self-relevant word conditions would have experienced higher levels of anxiety than subjects in the low nonself-relevant word conditions. Thus, the longer color-naming latencies in the low self-relevant word as opposed to the low nonself-relevant word conditions could have been due to greater anxiety in the former than in the latter conditions.

If this explanation of the reported effects was valid, we would expect to find increasing latency of color-naming response time with each additional exposure to a self-relevant word. Support for this notion comes from research (Bandura, 1969; Davison, 1968; Wine, 1971) showing that repeated exposure to anxiety-inducing stimuli produces increasingly severe anxiety reactions (unless these presentations are simultaneously paired with anxiety-reducing stimuli). Thus, an analysis of performance trends over trials should provide a reasonable test of the anxiety interpretation of the obtained results. Results of a trend analysis did not indicate the presence of any increase or decrease in latency of response time over trials for any condition. This suggests that an increased anxiety through exposure to self-relevant words interpretation of the results is not particularly viable.

We should also consider another alternative explanation. It might be argued that the roles adopted by subjects made them aware of the study's hypothesis and that they responded to the color-naming task accordingly. For example, Freedman (1969) has argued: "The data from role playing studies are people's guesses as to how they would behave if they were in a particular situation; they are not data on how they actually would behave and people's guesses as to future or hypothetical situations are not the stuff of which a science of human behavior is made [p. 114]." As it pertains to the present study, this position implies that the subjects' responses reflected their guesses about how people in the respective roles they assumed would perform on the Stroop Color-Word Test. Although this might explain the main effects for quantitative position and type of word, the probability that subjects were aware that these two variables were supposed to interact with each other seems highly unlikely. In other words, to account for the interaction between quantitative position and type of word, subjects would have to have been aware that color-naming latencies should be longer in the low self-relevant word conditions than in any other condition. We found no evidence that subjects held any such beliefs; hence, this alternative explanation also seems relatively untenable.

Finally, we might note that an inspection of Table 5.1 seems to indicate that the physical-prowess role had a stronger effect on latency of response time than did the other roles. However, the interaction between role, quantitative position, and type of word did not reach significance, and we have argued that the relationship between quantitative novelty and focus of attention should not depend on the particular property that defines level of novelty. Thus, the apparently stronger effect in the physical-prowess conditions warrants discussion.

One possible interpretation is that subjects who role played an individual with a small amount of motor skills were sensitized, if not overtly instructed, to respond slowly on the color-word task. This interpretation would explain the observed increase in response time for subjects in the low physical prowess self-relevant word condition, but it does not account for the fact that no such increase was found in the low physical-prowess nonself-relevant word condition. In other words, if the role indicated to subjects that they should respond slowly on the task, an increase in response time should have occurred regardless of the type of word used in the task.

In our opinion, a better explanation of the effect involves the fact that physical prowess is an extremely salient property. As Adams (1971) has pointed out, high levels of motor abilities are prerequisite for successful negotiation of the physical and social world. To the extent that he is correct, we would expect the property of physical prowess to be more salient than the other properties studied. This greater saliency could then cause this property to exert a greater effect on the focus of attention than the properties of wealth, power, and prestige. Thus, although quantitative position with regard to any property should affect the focus of attention, the salience of properties may also differ and, consequently, exert a greater or lesser impact.

6 Affect

Although the list of person-contributed factors that influence the attribution process (e.g., focus of attention) has grown, the literature is relatively silent regarding affective experience as a potential determinant of causal attribution. This is particularly striking in light of evidence that: (1) there is some agreement regarding the nature of affect; (2) affect is a ubiquitous component of cognitions; and (3) affect has been shown to influence basic cognitive processes such as memory and perception.

NATURE OF AFFECT

Affect is generally assumed to be an experience of internal activity as opposed to the perception of some quality inherent in external stimuli. It is typically equated with terms such as "feelings", "emotional arousal", and "mood." Alternatively, it has been conceptualized as an elemental internal state or process of physiological arousal. Irrespective of the nuances in its conceptualization, it is agreed that affect is an internal experience that has sign, or valence, and varies in intensity. The experience of affect can be either positive (pleasant) or negative (unpleasant), and the intensity of the experience ranges from high (very pleasant or unpleasant) to low (slightly pleasant or unpleasant).

AFFECT AND COGNITION

Not only is there agreement regarding the reality of experienced affect, but a substantial amount of research also indicates that cognitions of objects, events, people, etc., have affective components that vary in sign and intensity. For example, Osgood, Suci, and Tannenbaum (1957) find that cognitions of stimuli rated on the semantic differential consistently evidence three dimensions: evaluation *(E)*, potency *(P)*, and activity *(A)*. Noting the similarity between *E-P-A* and feelings/emotions, Osgood (1962, 1969) concludes that these dimensions represent the affective or emotional aspect of meaning. Explaining why the *E-P-A* dimensions appear to be pancultural (Osgood, 1964; Osgood, May, & Miron, 1975), Osgood (1969) states: "In my opinion, it is the innateness of the emotional reactions system of the human animal that underlies the universality of the affective E-P-A components of meaning [p. 195]."

Additional data relevant to the basic dimensions of affect come from Averill (1975). He obtained semantic differential ratings of over 500 words commonly associated with emotion (e.g., coy, loving, helpless). Factor analysis of these ratings yielded a clear pleasant–unpleasant dimension. Other studies on affect in language, despite their differing methodologies, have obtained what seems to be this same basic dimension. Bush (1972), for example, used multidimensional scaling of 264 adjectives judged by subjects to refer to feelings and found pleasant–unpleasant to be the primary dimension. By intercorrelating data obtained from multidimensional scaling, successive-intervals scaling (e.g., Bush, 1972), semantic differential scaling, and factor analysis of verbal self-report data (Mehrabian & Russell, 1974), Russell (1978) reports strong support for the convergent validity of the pleasant–unpleasant dimension of meaning. Osgood (1969) provides an appropriate context for interpreting the significance of these results and their implications for the relationship between affect and cognition: "In the human species these 'gut' reactions to things appear as the affective meaning systems (the E-P-A components of total meaning), and it is these components which provide us with what might most appropriately be called the 'feeling-tones' of concepts as part of their total meaning [p. 195]."

AFFECT AND COGNITIVE PROCESSES: PERCEPTION

Let us now consider the relationship between affect and perception and between affect and memory. Easterbrook (1959) has proposed that affect or emotion influences utilization of cues in the perceptual environment. Specifically, he reviews a large body of research indicating that increasing positive or negative emotional arousal narrows the field of attention and reduces the use of cues peripheral to a central task. Two studies illustrate the research on which Easterbrook's conclusions are based. In Bahrick, Fitts, and Rankin (1952), subjects either were offered bonuses (positive arousal) or were not offered bonuses (control) for superior performance on both a central task (visual tracking) and a secondary task (reporting the occurrence of light flashes on the periphery of the central display). Results indicated that subjects in the positive arousal condition exhibited superior performance on the central task but inferior performance on the secondary task relative to control subjects. Bursil (1958) reported similar results using a noxious stimulus (uncomfortable air temperature) to induce emotional arousal. The performance of negatively aroused subjects on a central task improved, but their performance on a peripheral task suffered relative to control subjects.

More recent studies continue to find this relationship between affective arousal and utilization of peripheral and central cues. In Bruning, Capage, Kozoh, Young, and Young (1968), subjects were first emotionally aroused by either a failure experience or by being observed by others. In both cases, the performance of aroused subjects on a central task was better than that of nonaroused subjects when peripheral cues were designed to mislead them and interfere with their performance on the central task (locating a target stimulus in a 7×7 matrix). When the peripheral cues were designed to facilitate solution of the central task, aroused subjects performed at a lower level than did nonaroused subjects. These results clearly indicate that arousal reduces subjects' use of peripheral cues.

Increased emotional arousal also decreases detection of peripheral differences between self and others (Firestone, Kaplan, & Russell, 1973) and the perception of peripheral material that immediately precedes or follows temporary arousal (Brenner, 1973); but it increases the utilization of cues associated with a central task, especially when the arousal is unexplained (Girodo, 1973). In an interesting variation on this theme, Konecni and Sargent-Pollock (1976) found that subjects aroused by a noxious stimulus while working on a difficult task select less complex intertask stimulation (a simple versus a complex melody) than do nonaroused subjects working on the same task. In explaining this effect, they argued that people realize the limits of their central processing systems (although subjects' ability to verbalize this realization was not tested). Therefore, under conditions of high emotional arousal, they realize they are less capable of dealing with complex intertask stimuli if they are to perform well on a difficult central task.

AFFECT AND COGNITIVE PROCESSES: MEMORY

The research reviewed indicates that affective arousal influences the process of perception under a wide variety of arousal manipulations and experimental tasks. It should not, therefore, be surprising that affectivity also influences other cognitive processes such as memory.

A recent theory of memory substitutes a "level of processing" approach (Craik & Lockhart, 1972) for the more traditional approach involving discrete categories of memory. In this model, the degree to which a stimulus is encoded and available for retrieval depends on the depth at which that stimulus is processed, rather than on whether the stimulus has characteristics that cause it to be transferred from primary to secondary short-term to long-term memory "boxes."

The major variable known to determine the depth at which a stimulus is processed is the meaningfulness of the cognition of that stimulus. As the meaningfulness of a given cognition increases, the depth at which it is processed and, thus, encoded and available for retrieval, increases. Given Osgood et al.'s (1957) conclusion that affectivity is a primary component of meaning, one would expect the affective sign and intensity associated with a given cognition to have a substantial impact on memory. This does, in fact, appear to be the case.

The role of affectivity in memory processes has been recognized for some time. Research begun in the early 1900s has found that positively and negatively valenced words are recalled faster than affectively neutral words; also, positively valenced words are recalled more quickly than those with negative valence. This relationship between affect and memory is apparently robust. It has been found with various types of memory tasks including paired associate (Keppel, 1963), serial (Anisfeld & Lambert, 1966), incidental memory-free recall (Amster, 1964), and instructed learning-free recall (Isen, Shalker, Clark, & Karp, 1978). In addition, Trimble and Brink (1969) provide evidence for the influence of affective intensity on memory. Using an incidental memory task, they found that CVC trigrams that were rated high in either positive or negative affective intensity were recalled 1 week after initial exposure to a greater extent than trigrams of moderate or low affective intensity.

It is also interesting to note that word affectivity interacts with self-esteem in the memory processes. People high in chronic self-esteem recall words that are affectively positive to a greater extent than words whose valence is negative; in contrast, people low in chronic self-esteem have better recall for negatively valenced than for positively valenced words (August, Rychlak, & Felker, 1975; Rychlak, Carlsen, & Dunning, 1974). Presumably this effect occurs because affectively positive material has more meaning for people high in self-esteem, whereas the reverse is true for people low in self-esteem. Thus, it seems clear that the affective sign and intensity associated with cognitive stimuli influence memory processes (although Holmes, 1970, has argued that the findings of increased memory for positive [pleasant] as opposed to negative [unpleasant] material occurs only when a substantial amount of time has elapsed between encoding and recall).

AFFECT AND ATTRIBUTION

Given the influence of affect on the cognitive processes of perception and memory, it seems reasonable to assume that affect plays a role in other cognitive processes including causal attribution. But why does the social psychological literature evidence a noticeable lack of interest in this potential relationship? Perhaps attribution theorists believe that Heider's (1944) axiom "good people do good things and bad people do bad things" adequately expresses the relationship between affect and attribution. Because a number of authors (e.g., Kelley, 1973) have expressed this point of view, a brief comparison between Heider's formula and our approach is in order.

The terms *good* and *bad* as used in Heider's hypothesis apparently connote evaluation; that is, the evaluator judges the worth of objective characteristics or qualities of stimuli against criteria such as normative prescriptions or an assessment of actual or potential benefit/harm to self. If a stimulus measures up to norms and/or is judged to be actually or potentially beneficial to self, the evaluator assigns a relatively stable linguistic label (i.e., *good*) to that stimulus. The label *bad* is assigned to stimuli not meeting the relevant criteria. Presumably, attribution for an event labeled *good* or *bad* proceeds in terms of locating a possible cause that is similarly labeled. Kelley (1973) provides an illustration of this label-matching attribution process: John dislikes Joe; John dislikes the meal Joe serves him. John attributes causality for the bad meal by finding a plausible cause that shares the label *bad*. In this case, Joe is labeled *bad* and would be seen as the cause. This model differs from our approach in several key respects.

The first major difference concerns the role of cognitive labels in the attribution process. People often label effects and events which may qualify as possible causes as *good* or *bad*. However, we assume that the experience or memory of experienced affect associated with events, rather than the labels *good* and *bad*, forms the basis for the influence of affect on causal attribution. Second, Heider's axiom suggests that affective sign (*good* versus *bad*) is the only variable concerning affect that is relevant to causal-attribution processes. We suggest that the intensity of affect as well as the affective sign associated with events will influence causal attribution.

Third, the labels *good* and *bad* connote affective experiences that remain relatively stable over time. This suggests that attribution based on affectivity would also remain stable over time. We see the influence of affectivity on causal attribution as being much more fluid. The affectivity associated with effects and events that may qualify as possible causes might change from situation to situation and from moment to moment, depending on factors such as the person's mood, contextual changes, memory processes, etc. Thus, affectively based causal attribution may also change over time and across situations.

EXPERIMENTAL HYPOTHESES

Having discussed the implications of the present conceptualization of affect in comparison to some previous thinking, it remains to derive hypotheses from application of the consistency principle to the affective dimension. In general, the consistency principle applied to affect suggests that the previously occurring event that meets both asymmetry criteria and is most similar to a given effect in terms of affectivity will be chosen as the cause of that effect. We can derive three more specific hypotheses from this general hypothesis.

First, the sign hypothesis states that there should be a strong tendency for individuals to attribute causality for some cognized effect to a cognized possible cause having the same affective sign as does the effect. Causality for an affectively positive, neutral, or negative effect should be attributed to a possible cause that shares the same affective sign.

The second hypothesis includes *affective intensity* as well as sign. As used here, the concept affective intensity simply means the magnitude of positive or negative affect (degree of pleasantness or unpleasantness) associated with a cognition. This hypothesis states that as the magnitude of the positive or negative affect associated with a cognized effect increases or decreases, the magnitude of the positive or negative affect of the cognized possible cause chosen as the cause for the effect should also increase or decrease. In other words, causality for a cognized effect experienced as very pleasant will tend to be attributed to a cognized possible cause also experienced as very pleasant; a moderately pleasant effect should be attributed to a moderately pleasant cause, and so forth (all other factors held constant).

The present experimental context also permits an empirical test of the second asymmetry criterion. Specifically, we have argued that attribution of causality for effects is limited to previously occurring events that qualify as possible causes for the effects. To qualify as a possible cause for an effect with regard to the dimension of affect, a cognized previously occurring event must be equal to or greater in affective intensity than the cognized effect (assuming that the events share affective sign). Thus, causality for effects should be attributed to cognized previously occurring events that are either equal to or greater, but not lesser, in affective intensity than are the cognized effects.

Research relevant to the present experimental hypotheses involves studies in which subjects are asked to attribute positive or negative effects to possible causes other than self. These findings are entirely consistent with the affective sign hypothesis. For example, Regan, Straus, and Fazio (1974) directly manipulated subjects' liking for a target person who then either succeeded or failed on a skilled task. The results indicate that success (the affectively positive effect) was attributed internally to the liked target person (an affectively positive possible cause). The disliked person's success was attributed to external factors (e.g., luck) rather than to the target person. This pattern was reversed when attributions were made for failure (a negative effect). In a second experiment (Regan et al., 1974), subjects were led to believe that either a liked or a disliked acquaintance of theirs had done a favor for another person (the effect). In attributing causality for this event, subjects again matched the affective signs of the possible causes and the effect. The favor (a positive effect) was attributed to the liked person. When the favor was apparently done by the disliked person, subjects attributed the action to external factors rather than to the person.

Similar results were found in two other studies (Feather & Simon, 1971; Frieze & Weiner, 1971). If subjects believed that an actor had succeeded on practice trials, they attributed continued success on the task to the actor and failure to factors external to the actor (e.g., luck). When subjects believed that the actor had failed on practice trials, they attributed continued failure to internal characteristics of the actor and success to external factors.

Finally, using the therapist-patient paradigm, Harvey, Arkin,

Gleason, and Johnston (1974) found evidence for affective matching of cause and effect by varying the sign of the therapeutic method. Specifically, in one set of conditions the method of therapy was described as generally reducing phobic patients' negative emotional reactions to the feared stimulus (an affectively positive possible cause). In a second set of conditions the method was described as generally ineffective in helping the phobic patients relax (an affectively negative possible cause). The results are consistent with the affective sign hypothesis. If the outcome of the therapist-patient interaction (either positive or negative) did not match the affective sign of the therapy program (provided by the experimenter), subjects attributed responsibility for the outcome to the therapist, an alternative possible cause. When the outcome matched the affective sign of the therapeutic program used, subjects attributed much less responsiblity for this outcome to the therapist and more responsibility to the program itself.

Although supporting the affective sign hypothesis, research concerning attribution for positive and negative effects to possible causes other than self evidences no attempt to explore the relationship between affect and attribution beyond Heider's (1944) axiom. In particular, we have been unable to find research relevant to the hypothesized tendency for people to select a possible cause for a given effect that is similar to that event in terms of affective intensity as well as sign. Therefore, the major purpose of the following study was to test the hypothesized relationships between affect and attribution suggested by the consistency principle.

A Test of the Hypotheses

In order to test the experimental hypotheses, effects differing in affective sign and intensity were necessary. The major methodological problem involved creating these conditions and minimizing the plausibility of a prior-learning interpretation of the results.

There is little doubt that people learn to associate certain effects with particular causes. This fact can and has been used to explain the relationship between affect and causal attribution (Kelley, 1973). Subjects see a particular effect event (X, which happens to be affectively valenced) and attribute causality for X to a specific event (A, which happens to be similarly valenced) because previous learning indicates that X is typically caused by A. Although this type of post hoc explanation cannot be excluded from consideration, it is possible to create conditions that minimize its plausibility as an alternative explanation.

The prior-learning approach assumes that people identify a particular effect's objective characteristics and then find the cause or type of cause that has covaried with that effect in the past. Therefore, any change in the affectivity of the effect that does not alter its objective characteristics should not affect the attribution of causality for that event. However, in terms of our approach, any change in the affectivity of the effect should produce a concomitant change in causal attribution. Therefore, utilizing methods that manipulate the affectivity of the effect without modifying its content would minimize the plausibility of a specific prior-learning alternative explanation for any given pattern of results.

Several methods might be used to alter the affectivity of the effect while holding the content of that event constant. For several reasons, the most reasonable option was altering the intensity of affect associated with the effect by making that effect a conditioned stimulus (CS) in a classical conditioning paradigm, using the onset or offset of aversive sound as the unconditioned stimulus (UCS). First, this technique has been used to establish an association between positive or negative affect and a particular stimulus (e.g., Zanna, Kiesler, & Pilkonis, 1970). Second, Grings (1973) specifies conditions that minimize the number of CS–USC pairings required to achieve conditioning. Given an appropriate cover story, minimizing the number of trials to conditioning should increase the unobtrusiveness of the manipulation and diminish the possibility of criticizing obtained effects on the grounds of experimental demand.

In order for conditioning to occur, Grings (1973) points out that the CS must elicit an orienting response. Because people tend to orient more to dynamic than to stable (unchanging) stimuli, the study used a dynamic social interation as the CS. Research also indicates that the orienting response is greater to unexpected than to expected stimulation. To take advantage of this phenomenon, the social interactions were videotaped and commenced suddenly after 25 seconds of blank videotape had been shown.

The second facilitator of conditioning (Grings, 1973) involves establishing a cognitive relationship between the CS and UCS through verbal instructions. The optimum method for creating this relationship is telling subjects that onset of the UCS will reliably follow onset of the CS (e.g., "every time the blue light comes on, a shock will follow"). Unfortunately, explicitly instructing subjects regarding onset of the CS and UCS in the context of the cover story used could produce undesirable side effects such as directing the subjects' attention to the details of the instructions and away from the experimental stimuli. To create some cognitive relationship between the aversive sound (UCS) and the social interaction (CS), subjects were told that the study involved the relationship between noise and the perception of cues in a social interaction situation.

Third, Grings (1973) states that increasing the certainty with which the onset of the CS predicts the onset of the UCS decreases trials to conditioning. Certainty is increased by holding the rate of association between onset of the CS and UCS constant, making the time interval between onset of the CS and UCS brief but constant, and holding the magnitude of the UCS constant across trials. The experimental procedure incorporated these principles as guidelines. The videotaped interaction sequences presenting the CS and UCS were shown twice; the experimenter told subjects that the *same* tape they had just seen would be shown a second time. The interval between onset of the CS and either onset or offset of the UCS was held constant at .5 seconds (an interstimulus interval that tends to maximize conditioning in human subjects). Also, the magnitude of the UCS was held constant.

Two specific criteria determined selection of the effect events. First, cognitions of these events had to be reliably associated with either positive, neutral, or negative affective signs. Second, the type of effect events that could be caused by numerous factors was needed so subjects would have a large pool of possible causes from which to choose, thereby increasing subjects' opportunities to make fairly subtle distinctions in terms of degree of affectivity in attributing causality for the effect. (This would facilitate determining the effect of the aversive sound manipulation on causal attribution.) Happily, Michotte (1950) describes the type of events that meets these two criteria.

As described in Chapter 2, Michotte's basic experimental paradigm for studying causal perception involves two small rectangles (A and B; 1 cm $\times$ .5 cm), which could be made to move along a horizontal slot (15 cm $\times$ .5 cm). The direction, extent, and speed of movement could be changed at will, allowing an infinite variety of kinetic combinations. In the course of experiments using this paradigm, Michotte (1950) noticed that subjects, without prompting, consistently interpreted the movements of the rectangles in affectively valenced terms. If, after A and B made contact, A remained stationary but B moved away rapidly, subjects consistently referred to these movements as an affectively negative interaction (e.g., "It is as though B was afraid of A and ran off", or "A joins B, then they fall out, have a quarrel, and B goes off by himself."). Reliably positive interpretations (characterized as a "gentle and friendly association" or even "a lovers' rendezvous") were given to the situation in which A and B made contact, paused, and moved off at the same slow, uniform speed and in the same direction while juxtaposed. When A and B simply appeared to pass one another, with or without pausing at the point of contact, subjects' reactions were affectively neutral (characterized as a "coincidental meeting"). Michotte (1950) suggests that the subjects' scenarios represent primitive emotional reactions to basic kinetic structures. Many psychologists have noted a similar tendency for individuals to interpret nonverbal behavior readily in emotional terms. It was felt that constructing social interaction sequences in terms of Michotte's kinetic guidelines would provide effects that would reliably produce affectively positive, negative, or neutral reactions. Also, these social interaction sequences represent common types of nonverbal social behavior often experienced by people and caused, in all probability, by many different factors.

Thus, although these archetypal social interactions were expected to produce positive, negative, or neutral impressions, these events would also impose minimal constraints on subjects' choice with regard to what could have reasonably caused the interactions to occur as they did. This would allow subjects to choose causes that vary in affective sign and intensity, a situation which improves the probability of detecting the more subtle effects of affect on causal attribution suggested by our theoretical position.

Choice of the dependent measure used in this experiment was determined by similar considerations. There are no sets of affectively valenced attributional categories equivalent to the ability, luck, effort, and task-difficulty items used extensively in current attribution research. Therefore, an open-ended measure asking subjects to choose a cause for the event they had just seen was used. This type of open-ended measure has yielded essentially the same results as the more structured, labeled type of scale (Nisbett, Caputo, Legant, & Maracek, 1973). An open-ended measure may in fact be preferable if the dimensions used by naive persons in making attributional judgments are not well-documented (Frieze, 1976).

Eighty-five male and female subjects participated in the experiment and were randomly assigned to conditions. Subjects participated in groups ranging in size from 8 to 11. To begin the experiment, subjects were seated at separate desks facing a TV monitor. Desks were situated to allow all subjects an unobstructed view of the screen.

The experimenter explained the nature and purpose of the study. He indicated that increasing attention is being paid to the effects of noise on the nervous system; however, little research had been directed toward understanding the relationship between noise and people's perception of social interactions. The importance of this, he continued, is evidenced in data showing substantial differences between typical understandings of social interactions in urban versus rural areas. He indicated that the differences in noise levels between these areas might, in part, account for the different styles of social interaction characteristic of urban and rural environments. The present study, he explained, is designed to investigate this possibility. At this point, the experimenter said:

For instance, we know that the interpretation of social interaction cues, such as movements and posture, affects the way a person reacts to that situation. We want to determine whether the level of background noise, or auditory distraction, affects interpretation of these cues, and, thus, affects the way a person reacts within such situations. The present experiment is designed to determine whether auditory distraction does affect the interpretation of cues present in a social interaction situation.

He then described the experimental procedures. First, subjects were told that they would be shown an actual social interaction between two students, which had been videotaped several weeks earlier. He indicated that subjects would be exposed to an auditory distractor, which had been added to the videotape by the research team. Subjects were then told that the taped interaction with its auditory distractor would be presented twice in order to insure that subjects attended to all significant aspects of the interaction. Subjects were then informed that after they had seen the taped interaction twice they would be questioned about their perceptions of the social interaction.

At this point, the experimenter turned on a videotape machine. In all conditions, the first 25 seconds of videotape were blank. Then the social interaction sequence appeared on the TV monitor. In all conditions, this interaction began with two men walking toward each other from opposite directions. They then stopped approximately 1.5 feet apart and appeared to engage in a brief (15 second) conversation. To increase the credibility of the interaction, a familiar area on the University of Southern California campus served as background. It is important to note that these interactions were videotaped (in black and white) from a distance of approximately 80 feet. The viewer could readily detect actors' gross body movements (e.g., speed and direction) but could not distinguish subtle postural changes, facial expressions, and so forth.

The kinetic structure of the social interactions was varied by altering the actions of the two people involved following the approach and pause that were common to all conditions. In the positive kinetic conditions, the two people walked away together. Following the pause in the neutral kinetic conditions, each person continued on in the direction he was originally going. In the negative kinetic conditions, one of the two people made a quick 180 degree turn (a sharp about-face) and hurriedly walked away while the second person remained stationary. In each case, the duration of the taped interaction was 20 seconds.

The kinetic structure manipulation was cross-cut by adding a three-level sound manipulation to the sound tracks of the videotapes. In two conditions the sound was aversive; low-level white noise was used in the third condition. The aversive sound was created by combining an 855 Hz tone with a 960 Hz tone played at 90 db, a stimulus rated as extremely unpleasant in pilot tests.

In the aversive sound onset conditions, onset of the previously described aversive sound occurred .5 seconds after the videotaped interaction appeared on the TV monitor and continued throughout the interaction (total of 19.5 seconds). In the offset conditions, the aversive sound began 6 seconds after the video-tape machine was turned on. This sound was terminated .5 seconds after the videotaped interaction appeared on the monitor (total of 19.5 seconds). In the neutral sound conditions, the onset of low-level white noise (30 db) occurred at the same time as the onset of the videotaped interaction sequence and was terminated at the end of that presentation (total of 20 seconds). It should be noted that in each condition subjects were exposed to 25 seconds of blank videotape, 20 seconds of social interaction, 19.5 seconds of aversive sound (in the two aversive sound conditions), and 20 seconds of white noise (in the neutral sound conditions).

Following the videotaped presentation, the experimenter told subjects that his research team intercepted both people involved in the interaction after the filming was completed. They supposedly interviewed both people concerning the topic of their interaction, what was actually said, and why the interaction had taken place. The experimenter said:

> What we would like you to do is to write down in your own words what you believe to be the topic of the interaction you just saw, and what you think the two people said to one another. We would also like you to choose a factor or factors from your own memory and experience which you think might have caused the interaction to happen as it did.

Following these instructions, the experimenter explained that after he had gathered these data from about 100 subjects, all subjects' impressions of what happened and why it happened would be compared with the data gathered from the people who had engaged in the interaction. He said that this comparison would indicate whether auditory distraction affects the interpretation of cues in a social interaction.

At this point, the experimenter distributed index cards to each subject while he repeated the instructions to: (1) write in their own words what they believed to be the topic and content of the taped interaction and (2) describe in their own words their choice of a factor or factors that they believed might have caused the interaction to happen as it did. No time limit for responding was imposed on the subjects. After collecting these data, the experimenter thanked the subjects for their participation and dismissed them.

Unfortunately, sufficient numbers of subjects were not available to permit several sessions to be run for each experimental condition. But any bias that could have resulted from this fact was minimized in the following ways. First, instructions to the subjects were identical for all conditions and were simply read by the experimenter. Second, the experimental manipulations were presented entirely on videotape. Third, the experimenter was blind to condition until he turned on the videotape machine. Finally, no interaction, verbal or otherwise, was permitted among subjects during the course of the experimental session.

For purposes of statistical analysis, it was necessary to obtain ratings of the degree of pleasantness or unpleasantness associated with each subject's response on the open-ended measures. In order to accomplish this, independent judges trained in this rating task and blind to the experimental hypotheses and manipulations were used. These four judges rated the open-ended responses obtained from each of the 85 subjects in terms of the degree of pleasantness–unpleasantness inherent in the choices of cause and in the descriptions of the events. For purposes of analysis, judges' ratings of the events and causes using -3 to $+3$ scales were transformed into ratings ranging from 1 (very unpleasant) to 7 (very pleasant). The interjudge reliabilities were high for ratings of the event descriptions (r's ranged from .70 to .81) and for ratings

TABLE 6.1
Frequencies of Cause and Effect Affective
Sign Combinations

	Sign of Cause		
Sign of Event	Positive	Neutral	Negative
Positive	113	48	27
Neutral	24	39	25
Negative	12	16	36

of causal choices (r's ranged from .73 to .84); judges' ratings were summed for analysis.

If the consistency principle as applied to the affective dimension is valid, the sign of the affect associated with an event should match the affective sign of that event's cause regardless of the experimental condition from which the causes and effects are drawn. Inspection of the cell frequencies in a 3 (kinetic structure) × 3 (sound) × 4 (judges) contingency table showed no evidence of any interaction between judges. Therefore, for purposes of analysis, the frequency data were collapsed over judges (Table 6.1). The results of a chi-square analysis of these data clearly confirm predictions. Subjects were more likely to choose a cause with the same affective sign as the event than a cause with a sign that differed from that of the event, $\chi^2 (4) = 66.40$, $p < .001$.

To determine whether the experimental manipulations had the intended effect on perceived affectivity of the events, analyses were carried out on the judges' ratings of subjects' event descriptions (Table 6.2). The results of this analysis reveal the predicted main effects for kinetic structure, $F (2, 76) = 32.99$, $p < .001$, and for sound, $F (2, 76) = 3.47$, $p < .05$. An inspection of these data indicates that in general subjects in the positive kinetic conditions saw the event as more positive than subjects in the neutral or negative kinetic conditions. Subjects in the offset conditions generally saw the event as more positive (in the positive and neutral kinetic conditions) and less negative (in the negative kinetic conditions) than subjects in the neutral and onset sound conditions. Planned comparisons using the Newman-Keuls procedure were

TABLE 6.2
Mean Ratings of Event Descriptions

Sound		Kinetic Structure		
		Positive	Neutral	Negative
Offset	M	23.00_a	19.09_b	15.18_c
	n	8	11	11
Neutral	M	20.67_{ab}	18.60_b	11.12_d
	n	9	10	8
Onset	M	18.75_b	18.70_b	15.00_c
	n	8	10	10

Note: As mean values increase, rated positiveness increases. Means with common subscripts do not differ significantly.

carried out to define the components of these main effects further. The results of this analysis indicate that the primary component of the main effect for kinetics is the difference between rated affectivity of events in the positive and negative kinetic conditions ($p <$ .05). The main effect for sound reflects significant differences between the positive kinetic-offset and positive kinetic-onset conditions ($p < .05$) and between the negative kinetic-offset and negative kinetic-neutral conditions ($p < .05$).

Given that the manipulation of event affectivity was generally successful, the consistency principle predicts that the affectivity of the cause will vary as a function of the affectivity of the effect (i.e., the social interaction). As previously noted, judges' ratings were highly correlated (r's ranging from .73 to .84) and were summed for analysis. An analysis of these data (Table 6.3) reveals the predicted main effect for kinetic structure, $F(2, 76) = 15.28, p <$ .001, and for sound, $F(2, 76) = 3.38, p < .05$. No interaction was obtained.

Planned comparisons using the Newman-Keuls procedure indicate that the patterns of these main effects are generally in the predicted direction. Subjects in the positive and neutral kinetic conditions tended to choose causes that were more positive in affective valence than did subjects in the negative kinetic conditions ($p < .05$), although no substantial differences between the positive and neutral kinetic structure conditions were evident. Also as predicted, subjects in the offset conditions generally chose causes that were more positive (in the positive and neutral kinetic conditions) and less negative (in the negative kinetic conditions) than did subjects in the neutral or onset sound conditions. This tendency is primarily reflected in the significant differences between the positive kinetic-offset and positive kinetic-onset conditions ($p <$ .05) combined with the difference between the negative kinetic-offset and negative kinetic-neutral conditions ($p < .05$). It should be pointed out, however, that the significant difference between the negative kinetic-neutral and negative kinetic-onset conditions is in a direction opposite to prediction. Subjects in the negative kinetic-onset condition chose causes that were less affectively negative than causes chosen by subjects in the negative kinetic-neutral condition. Ironically, this deviation from prediction may have come about as a result of the previously discussed relationship between emotional arousal and utilization of peripheral cues. For instance, the critical aspect of the negative kinetic manipulation is the rapid movement of one person away from the other. If this movement is treated as a peripheral cue and subjects in the negative kinetic-onset condition were emotionally aroused by the onset of the aversive sound, they may have underutilized this cue in forming an impression of the affectivity of the event. Underutilization of this negative peripheral cue could have led subjects in this condition to form a less negative impression than

TABLE 6.3
Mean Ratings of Cause Responses

Sound		Kinetic Structure		
		Positive	Neutral	Negative
Offset	M	23.00_a	18.73_b	15.73_{bc}
	n	8	11	11
Neutral	M	20.00_{ab}	17.20_{bc}	11.00_d
	n	9	10	8
Onset	M	18.38_b	17.80_{bc}	14.40_c
	n	8	10	10

Note: As mean values increase, rated positiveness increases. Means with common subscripts do not differ significantly.

emotionally nonaroused subjects in the negative kinetic-neutral sound condition. It is also possible that the combination of aversive sound and the negative interaction resulted in a "defensive denial" effect; subjects may have tuned out these negative cues, producing less negative ratings in this condition.

The first two hypotheses predict that the ratings of the affective sign and intensity associated with the cause should match the sign and intensity of the effect. The third hypothesis predicts that the affective intensity of the cause will be greater than, if not equal to, that of the effect. In other words, if the event is rated $+2$ (moderately positive), the rating of the cause of that event should either match the affectivity of the event (i.e., receive a $+2$ rating also) or exceed the rating of the event in affective intensity (i.e., receive a $+3$, very positive, rating). The cause should not be perceived as having less affective intensity than the effect (i.e., receive a $+1$ or 0 rating).

In order to test this hypothesis, the frequency of cases in which the cause was rated as being equal to or greater than the affective intensity of the effect was computed. Next, the frequency of cases in which the cause was rated as less intensely affective than the effect was computed. This latter case included those instances in which the affective sign of the cause and the effect differed. These frequencies were then compared against cell frequencies that would have occurred by chance. This analysis confirmed the hypothesis. In 214 instances, the intensity of affect associated with the cause was equal to or greater than the affective intensity of the effect; in only 126 cases was the perceived cause rated as less affectively intense than the effect, $\chi^2 (1) = 4.66$, $p < .05$.

The hypotheses generated by applying the consistency principle to the dimension of affect received clear support in terms of subjects' open-ended responses. Subjects were much more likely to attribute causality for the social interaction events to possible causes that shared the affective sign of those events than they were to possible causes that did not match the effects in affective sign. Subjects exposed to a positive social interaction chose causes for that event that were more positive than were causes chosen by subjects exposed to a negative social interaction. There was also a tendency for subjects exposed to an affectively positive or negative interaction to choose causes that were more positive or negative than those chosen by subjects exposed to an affectively neutral interaction.

In general, the affective intensity of the causes also varied as a function of the affective intensity of the social interaction. Increasing or decreasing the magnitude of positive affect associated with the positive social interaction tended to increase or decrease the magnitude of the positive affect associated with the chosen cause of the interaction. Decreasing the magnitude of negative affect associated with the negatively valenced interaction tended to decrease the magnitude of negative affect associated with the cause of this interaction. The unsuccessful attempt to increase the negativity of the negatively valenced interaction makes it impossible to determine whether this would influence causal attribution in the predicted manner. Likewise, the failure to alter substantially the affective magnitude of the neutral social interaction prevents generalization of the present theoretical formulation to effect events that are associated with neutral affectivity.

The hypothesis generated by the second asymmetry criterion also received support. Subjects were more likely to select causes associated with a level of affective intensity (either positive or negative) that was equal to or greater than that of the interaction event than they were to choose causes of lesser affective intensity than the interaction event.

Alternative Explanations

Before considering the implications of this study, the relationship between our theoretical approach and other attributional theories dealing with affect should be considered in light of these experimental results. As previously noted, Kelley's (1967, 1971, 1973) model of causal attribution assumes that people base attributions on prior learning if sufficient covariation data are absent. If a person observes an effect (X) and has learned that X is usually caused by A, he or she will attribute the cause for X to A. From Kelley's perspective, subjects' attributions in the foregoing experiment would have resulted from their having previously learned that the social interactions as presented in the particular experimental context are typically caused by certain events.

Our approach is quite different. Although not completely discounting the impact of prior learning on attribution, it is assumed that causal attribution is essentially a dynamic process of cognitive organization. When asked to attribute causality for an effect, the individual attributes causality to the possible cause that is most consistent with the effect. This approach predicts that causality will be attributed to the possible cause that is more similar to the effect on all relevant dimensions than are other possible causes.

The experimental results seem to favor our approach. Although subjects may have learned previously that the positive, neutral, or negative social interaction has a positive, neutral, or negative cause, it is difficult to believe they had learned that events accompanied by the offset of aversive sound are generally caused by events that are more positive or less negative than events accompanied by white noise or the onset of aversive sound. The nature of the social interaction further reduces the plausibility of attribution based on prior learning. The use of events that could be caused by multiple factors reduces the subject's ability to use prior learning as a specific guideline in determining causality. It should be noted, however, that it seems impossible to completely rule out the form of the prior-learning interpretation based on generalization as a post hoc alternative explanation for any obtained pattern of results.

Heider's balance model (1958) as elaborated by Insko, Songer, and McGarvey (1974) is also tangentially relevant to the relationship between affect and causal attribution. In Insko et al.'s analysis, the overall degree of balance in a p-o-x configuration is an additive function of the degree of balance within each separate band of this configuration (i.e., p-o, p-x, o-x) and the degree of balance between separate bands (i.e., p-x versus o-x), as well as the three-band balance emphasized by Heider (1958). Insko et al. use this model to predict the degree of balance in the eight possible p-o-x configurations as measured by subjects' ratings of the pleasantness–unpleasantness of the various configurations. For instance, a p-o-x configuration in which p likes o and p and o both like or dislike x has three units of balance: p's positive attitude toward o is a balanced p-o band; the p-x and o-x bands are balanced because p and o have similar attitudes toward x; finally, the three-band component is balanced. Alternatively, a p-o-x configuration in which p dislikes o but both p and o like or dislike x has only one unit of balance: the agreement between p and o regarding x. Thus, Insko et al. predict and find that the former configuration is perceived as more pleasant than the latter presumably because it is more balanced.

The relevance of this formulation to affect and attribution involves certain assumptions about the generality of the p-o-x balance model. First, it must be assumed that the perceived affectivity of the social interactions in this experiment can be equated with the sentiment relationship between p and o in the p-o-x model. Second, it must be assumed that subjects typically believed that the interaction between the two people in the videotape involved some sentiment relation with an x (an object, event, person, etc., common to both people). Third, it must be assumed that the subjects' belief in the people's sentiment relation with a common x would be expressed in their descriptions of the causes for the social interaction. Given these assumptions, balance theory could make certain predictions regarding the affectivity of the cause chosen for the events as a function of the affectivity of the social interaction events. For instance, if subjects perceived the social interaction as positive, balance theory predicts that they would also assume that p and o's sentiment relation regarding a common x would be in agreement because assumed agreement produces a more balanced p-o-x configuration if the relationship between p and o is positive. The presence of this assumed agreement in the description of the cause would most probably lead judges to rate the cause positively because agreement is generally perceived as more positive than disagreement. Therefore, balance theory could predict that a subject's choice of a cause for a positive event would be positive due to the individual's tendency to construct the most balanced p-o-x configuration possible within the limitations of the situation.

However, when the affectivity of the interaction is negative, predictions derived from balance theory diverge from those of the present model. When the relationship between p and o is negative, balance theory predicts no preference for a p-o-x configuration in which p and o agree or disagree regarding x. In fact, when subjects believe that the relationship between p and o is negative and that p and o will have contact in the future, data reported by Insko et al.

indicate that subjects prefer a *p-o-x* configuration in which *p* and *o* agree regarding *x*. Translated into an attributional context, this finding suggests that subjects in the negative interaction conditions would tend to mention agreement rather than disagreement in describing the cause of the interaction—content that should result in a positive or neutral rating of the cause on a scale ranging from "very positive" to "very negative". Our model predicted and found the opposite tendency. When the social interaction was perceived as negative, the affectivity of the cause was given a clearly negative rating.

Another possibility should be considered. In one variation of the experimental procedures used by Insko et al., subjects were told that *p* and *o* had social contact in the past but would not have contact in the future. Under these conditions, subjects preferred a *p-o-x* configuration in which *p* and *o* disagreed regarding *x* rather than a *p-o-x* configuration in which *x* was agreed upon when the relationship between *p* and *o* was negative. If subjects in the present experiment believed that the people in the negative interaction conditions had contact in the past but would not in the future, balance theory could predict descriptions of the interaction in terms suggesting disagreement—descriptions that would presumably be rated negatively by the judges. To determine whether this variation of the *p-o-x* model played any role in determining the results of the present experiment, subjects' descriptions of the negative interaction were divided into three groups: those implying future contact between two people; those implying no future contact; and those in which the implications for future contact were ambiguous. Only 4 of the 29 descriptions of the negative interaction clearly implied no future contact, 15 clearly implied future contact, and 10 were ambiguous. A comparison of the judges' ratings of the no future contact group's choice of causes ($M = 12.25$) with ratings of causes from the future contact group ($M = 14.53$) indicates no significant difference ($t < 1$). Combining the no future contact and ambiguous groups ($M = 13.35$) in comparison with the future contact group also yields no significant difference ($t < 1$). This suggests that the consistency principle represents a better general theoretical basis for the results of the present experiment than does Insko et al.'s extension of the *p-o-x* balance model.

IMPLICATIONS

The present study is relevant to a number of extant psychological phenomena. For example, Dion, Berscheid, and Walster (1972) suggest that people are stereotyped in terms of their level of physical attractiveness. A person high in physical attractiveness is perceived as possessing behavior-relevant characteristics that are higher in social desirability (e.g., intelligence, parental competence) than is an unattractive person. The study by Dion et al. as well as a study by Dermer and Thiel (1975) found support for this hypothesis. But, our approach suggests that this effect may be an attributional rather than a stereotyping phenomenon. For instance, people high in physical attractiveness are probably associated with greater positive affect than are people low or moderate in attractiveness (other person-relevant information held constant). The affect associated with behavior-relevant characteristics probably also varies as a function of the social desirability of those characteristics. Assuming that behaviors implied by characteristics are effects and that the attractive or unattractive person is a possible cause, our results suggest that subjects would attribute characteristics to people in accordance with the consistency principle. As the attractiveness of the person increases, the social desirability of characteristics attributed to that person would also increase—precisely the pattern of results now explained in terms of a "beautiful is good" stereotype.

Related evidence from several studies (e.g., Miller, 1970) concerns the attribution of causality as a function of attractiveness. General findings are that causality for good outcomes is assigned to attractive people, whereas unattractive people are seen as responsible for bad outcomes. Given that attractive people are more affectively positive possible causes than are unattractive people, the present theoretical approach would also predict these findings.

Turning to another substantive area, our approach also offers an alternative explanation for the tendency of frustrated people to aggress against disliked others to a greater extent than against liked others (Berkowitz & Knurek, 1969). Specifically, Berkowitz (1971, 1974) argues that an individual who is frustrated or otherwise subjected to aversive stimulation is more prone to aggress than a person who is not exposed to such stimulation. However, elicitation of actual aggression requires the presence of a stimulus that has aggressive meaning—meaning that the stimulus acquired by virtue of being associated with harm to others. Berkowitz (1971, 1974) further argues that a disliked person has, as a stimulus, more agressive meaning than does a liked person. Therefore, a disliked person is more likely to elicit an aggressive response from a person primed to aggress than is a liked person.

The present approach would interpret this phenomenon in different terms. Dollard, Doob, Miller, Mowrer, and Sears (1939) originally proposed that the preferred target of aggression is the perceived cause of frustration (provided that no inhibitions regarding aggressing against that cause are present). If frustration or exposure to aversive stimuli causes negative affect, our approach predicts that the person will attribute this affect to a possible cause that is also negatively valenced. Disliked people fall into this category. Therefore, the person perceives the disliked person (on some level) as the cause of negative affect and thus aggresses against that person.

The present results are also applicable to misattribution phenomena. A number of researchers have found that subjects will misattribute mild, but not intense, fear (Nisbett & Schachter, 1966; Ross, Rodin, & Zimbardo, 1969) and anxiety (Singerman, Borkovec, & Baron, 1976) to a stimulus that did not actually cause the negative affect. The concept of plausible cause is typically used to explain this finding. As noted by Nisbett and Schachter (1966), the causes provided within the experimental situation (e.g., placebo pills, aversive noise) may serve as plausible causes for mildly negative affect but are implausible causes for intense fear or anxiety. Our approach provides a theoretical basis for this explanation. Subjects will attribute mildly negative affect to a possible cause (e.g., an ingested placebo) that they believe will produce mildly negative side effects because the effect and possible cause are similar in affective sign and intensity. On the other hand, subjects are unwilling to attribute intensely negative affect to a previously occurring event associated with mildly negative side effects because that event violates the second asymmetry criterion.

In other words, subjects experiencing intense levels of negative affect reject the previously occurring event (e.g., an ingested placebo) as a possible cause because intensity of negative affect associated with the previously occurring event is less than the intensity of negative affect associated with the effect. However, if the side effects of the placebo were, for example, described as intensely negative (e.g., nausea, trembling), subjects experiencing intensely negative affect should attribute causality to this stimulus just as subjects experiencing mildly negative affect attribute causality to a stimulus that presumably produces mildly negative side effects.

The possibility of reinterpreting the "beautiful is good" effect, one aspect of Berkowitz's (1971, 1974) model of aggression, and some effects or lack of effects in misattribution research in terms of the consistency principle applied to the dimension of affect suggest that affect plays a major role in attribution. On a more general level, the present model could partially restore the deterministic status of attitudes in goal-directed models of behavior. For example, our approach treats affect as a component of cognitions. Thurstone (1929) defines an attitude as the case in which affect is associated with a stimulus, a definition endorsed by Fishbein (1967). The similarities between the two treatments of affect suggest that the present study could be reconceptualized as a study concerning the impact of attitudes on causal attribution. To the extent that a person has a positive or negative attitude toward some effect, he or she will tend to attribute causality for that effect to a possible cause associated with an attitude of similar affective sign and intensity. To the extent that causal attribution influences behavior, attitudes would indirectly influence behavior by influencing the attribution process. The attributional reinterpretation of the influence that attitudes exert on aggression is one example illustrating the viability of this proposition, and future research would do well to investigate the extent to which behaviors are influenced by attitudes via the mechanism of causal attribution.

7

Defensive Attribution

Our theory of causal attribution as articulated and applied to the dimensions of time, space, focalization, and affect implies that the only factor that "biases" causal attribution is the motive to maximize simplicity within consciousness. This state of affairs leaves us slightly uneasy. In particular, the theory we have presented suggests that a person would not hesitate to attribute a negative event (e.g., failure) to self if this attribution were in line with the consistency principle. In fact, in Chapter 2 we present data indicating that people will attribute very negative events to self if the focalization of self is increased (Duval, Duval, & Neely, 1979). However, experience indicates that we often attribute a negative outcome to external causes when the consistency principle calls for an attribution to self.

Federoff and Harvey (1976) provide an excellent example of this phenomenon. In the experiment, subjects were led to believe that their task performance would be followed by either success or failure. Thus, temporal and spatial similarity between the subjects and the task outcome was constant for all conditions. Also, no manipulation regarding the affective sign/intensity of the subject's self was included; therefore, all subjects were equally similar (or dissimilar) to the task outcome on the affective dimension. However, the degree of focalization associated with the cognition of self was increased for half of the subjects by pointing a TV camera toward them. Because similarities and differences between the subjects and the task outcome regarding the dimension of time, space, and affectivity were held constant, subjects in the camera conditions should have attributed more causality to self for success and for failure than subjects in the no-camera conditions. This did not occur. Subjects in the camera conditions attributed more causality for success to self but *less* causality for failure to self than did subjects in the no-camera conditions. This is not an isolated example of the tendency to attribute success internally and failure externally (see Bradley, 1978; Jones, 1973; Miller & Ross, 1975, for reviews).

The frequency with which individuals attribute negative events externally when an internal attribution is, theoretically, more appropriate has generated the concept *defensive attribution*. Typically, this effect is explained in terms of the need for moderately high self-esteem (Rogers, 1959) and the existence of some mechanism akin to the ego, which protects the person's self-esteem by redirecting causality for negative events away from self. If this were the case, how could anyone be low in self-esteem unless they were in some sense psychologically deficient or abnormal? Thus, we cannot endorse this particular type of explanation for defensive attribution. However, the phenomenon itself is real and must be taken into account in a theory of causal attribution. Ideally, we would like to integrate this phenomenon in terms of the general theory. But, for the moment, we must be content with trying to determine the circumstances under which defensive attribution does and does not occur.

First, let us assume that the human organism is put together so that when interacting with the world its first tendency is to cope with, rather than to avoid, the problems, threatening situations, and so on that exist in that world. This assumption seems reasonable because a reversal in behavioral priorities (i.e., avoidance before coping) would probably shorten the person's life span considerably.

Second, let us assume that people believe that their causal attributions are accurate and facilitate successfully coping with the world (again, not an unreasonable position to take). True, locating causality for a problem in self rather than externally would probably result in the unpleasant experience of lowered self-esteem. However, we assume that this decline in feelings of self-worth would be offset by the anticipated solution of the problem and the concomitant restoration of self-esteem. Accordingly, we conclude that a person trying to cope with a problem wants to know the cause even if it is located in self. For example, suppose that an interpersonal relationship that you value is disintegrating. You believe your causal-attribution processes are accurate, but those processes locate the cause of the problem in you. Although this attribution for the problem to self lowers your self-esteem at that time, the belief that this knowledge will help you cope with the problem and restore or even enhance the relationship would, in all probability, outweigh your temporary discomfort. Therefore, the tendency first to cope with problems rather than to avoid them plus the belief that knowledge of causality aids coping should encourage you to accept attribution of the problem to self.

We have argued that the motivation to cope would encourage the acceptance of causal attributions. However, we should point out that the acceptance of a self-attribution for a negative event is probably based on some cost–benefit analysis (we imply no conscious use of a hedonic calculus or the like) which indicates that the benefits of accepting the self-attribution are greater than the costs and that the costs of avoiding this attribution (i.e., no solution) are greater than the benefits (i.e., maintenance of self-esteem). It should be clear that this cost–benefit analysis results in the acceptance of a negative self-attribution only if people believe they are capable of coping with the problem once the cause of that problem is known. If people believe they cannot cope with the problem, the costs of accepting the negative self-attribution become greater than the benefits; self-esteem is lowered without any reasonable expectation of solving the problem and restoring self-esteem. Similarly, the benefits of avoiding the attribution to self are probably greater than the costs. Making an external attribution for the problem maintains self-esteem, and the negative impact of the problem's presence can be reduced by distancing oneself from the problem and/or conditions associated with that problem.

Returning to the previous example, if you locate the cause of the disintegrating relationship in self, but feel that you cannot reduce or eliminate that problem, self-attribution would be associated with the cost of lowered self-esteem, but there would be no possibility of future, offsetting benefits. Alternatively, attributing responsibility for the problem externally rather than internally protects self-esteem, and one can reduce the negative impact of the disintegrating relationship by distancing oneself from that situation. This suggests that the extent to which people believe they can cope with a particular problem is a critical variable in determining whether defensive attribution will occur. An attribution of the problem to self will be accepted to the extent that people believe they can cope. To the extent that they believe they cannot resolve the problem, they will engage in defensive attribution (i.e., an attribution to factors other than self).

There is some evidence consistent with our analysis of the conditions under which defensive attribution will and will not occur. For example, in Duval et al. (1979) subjects were given specific ways to help reduce or eliminate the negative effects for which they were asked to attribute responsibility (either the plight of venereal disease victims or poverty in Latin America); they could volunteer time, money, and effort. Under these circumstances, increasing self-focus increased self-attribution, and there was no evidence of defensive attribution. However, in the study by Federoff and Harvey (1976), subjects knew they would be given only one opportunity to administer therapy to a phobic. Under these conditions, defensive attribution for failure to produce improvement in the phobic's condition was clearly in evidence, and increasing self-focus increased the tendency to attribute defensively. Thus subjects given ways to cope (Duval et al., 1979) did not engage in defensive attribution, whereas subjects without the possibility of further coping (Federoff & Harvey, 1976) attributed causality for the negative event externally. Of course, the two studies were quite different except for the self-focus manipulation, and research is needed in which the ability to cope is specifically manipulated. In the following section, we report two studies that were designed with this issue in mind.

COPING ABILITY AND DEFENSIVE ATTRIBUTION

In the first study, subjects were led to believe that they had a deficiency in a moderately important intellectual ability. They were told that they either could or could not eliminate this problem by working on a remedial task. In order to generate data comparable to those of Federoff and Harvey (1976), subjects' levels of self-focus either were or were not increased by use of a videotape camera. In order to measure subjects' attribution for the negative affect associated with the deficiency unobtrusively, subjects' self-esteem and their evaluations of the experiment and the experimenter were assessed before and after the critical manipulations. We assumed that a decrease in self-esteem would reflect attribution of the negative event to self; increasingly negative evaluations of the experiment and/or experimenter were assumed to reflect defensive attribution. In terms of our analysis, subjects in the cannot-reduce conditions were expected to evaluate the experimenter and/or the experimental situation more negatively after than before the manipulation. Their levels of self-esteem should remain stable from the first to the second measure. Conversely, we expected the self-esteem of subjects in the can-reduce conditions to be more negative after the manipulation than before. Their evaluations of the experimenter and/or the experimental situation should not change as a function of time of measurement. Further, we expected increased self-focus to accentuate these effects because the negativeness of intraself discrepancies such as intellectual deficiencies is increased by self-focus (Duval, Jellison, & Woodward, 1978). Therefore, subjects in the can-reduce camera condition should be lower in self-esteem than subjects in the can-reduce no-camera condition. In the cannot-reduce conditions, subjects should have more reason to engage in defensive attribution in the camera than in the no-camera condition. This increased tendency to attribute defensively should result in a more negative evaluation of the experimenter and/or the experimental situation.

Fifty-six male students participated in the study. They were randomly assigned to one of four conditions in a 2 (can/cannot-reduce) × 2 (camera/no-camera) factorial design. The experimenters met individually with each subject. After entering the experimental cubicle, the subject was greeted by two male experimenters (*A* and *B*) and was seated in front of a TV monitor. *B* introduced himself and told the subject that the study involved taking a short test that would be scored by computer. In all conditions, this interaction between *B* and the subject lasted for 2 to 3 minutes. *B* then introduced experimenter *A* who explained that he was a graduate student hired by the psychology department to carry out an evaluation program. He indicated that the department was interested in determining how experiments affect subjects' mood and how subjects feel about the experiments and experimenters. He said that the psychology department had constructed a set of three questionnaires that he would administer to the subject at three different points during the study. He explained that the first questionnaire of each set would assess the subject's mood. The second and third questionnaires would ask the subject to evaluate this particular experiment and experimenter (pointing to experimenter *B*). He emphasized that the subject's responses to these questionnaires would be completely confidential. Pointing to a padlocked box, he told the subject to slide his completed questionnaires through the slit in the lid and explained that four faculty members on the experiment review board would have sole access to the subject's responses. The subject was urged to be as candid as possible in his responses. Experimenter *A* then handed the first set of questionnaires to the subject for completion. At this point, both experimenters left the room; *B* said he would return in about 10 minutes.

The three questionnaires in each set were labeled "Mood Adjective Checklist", "Evaluation of the Experimental Environment", and "Evaluation of the Experimenter". Each questionnaire was made up of 14 items. Each item was accompanied by a 20-point scale, anchored with the terms *extremely appropriate* and *extremely inappropriate*. The mood questionnaire was actually designed to measure the subject's self-esteem and consisted of items such as *masterful, trustworthy,* and *intelligent.* The questionnaire labeled as an evaluation of the experimental environment was made up of items such as *comfortable, interesting,* and *attractive.* The third questionnaire asked the subject to evaluate the experimenter and included items such as *pleasant, efficient,* and *courteous.*

After approximately 10 minutes, experimenter *B* returned and began by explaining the purpose of the study in detail. He told the subject that the study was sponsored by the National Institute for the Study of Intellectual Abilities and was designed to determine whether the subject had a deficiency in mental ability known as Collier's syndrome. *B* handed the subject a pamphlet supposedly prepared by the Institute to explain the nature of this research. According to this pamphlet, the study was part of a nationwide effort to diagnose and, when possible, to remedy a deficiency in the ability to make quantitative judgments in three dimensions. It identified this deficiency as Collier's syndrome. The pamphlet went on to say that this type of judgment, although not absolutely essential to functioning in the world, could affect a person's performance on a variety of intellectual tasks. The pamphlet explained that the subject would be given a computer-controlled diagnostic test to determine if he had Collier's syndrome. (All subjects were led to believe that they had this deficiency.) If the diagnostic test found that he did suffer from Collier's syndrome, the computer would further analyze his pattern of responses to determine whether or not he had the potential to eliminate this deficiency by participating in a remedial program developed by the Institute. Because the subject's belief that he could or could not eliminate this deficiency was the critical variable in terms of our theoretical analysis, the pamphlet went on at some length to convince the subject that the diagnostic test was essentially 100% accurate. This part of the pamphlet read:

> By potential to eliminate Collier's syndrome, we do not mean simply a possibility of remedy. Over 5 years of extensive testing and evaluation have proved that we have achieved a level of accuracy in determining the presence of Collier's syndrome and the potential for eliminating Collier's syndrome that is practically without parallel in the psychological world. If the computer indicates that you have the potential to improve, it means that with your active and attentive participation in our program your deficiency will be completely eliminated within a relatively short period of time. If the diagnostic test indicates that you have Collier's syndrome but do not have the potential to eliminate the deficiency, you may, if you wish, participate in our program although there is almost no possibility that the syndrome can be reduced.

To enhance the credibility of the cover story, the experimenter explained to the subject that if the diagnostic test indicated he did not have Collier's syndrome, he would be dismissed with full credit. The subject was then informed that participation in the study was completely voluntary. Seven subjects chose not to continue their participation, behavior which is interesting in itself. If the subject chose to continue, the experimenter said that he would like to go over a few details before administering the test.

He first explained that quantitative judgment in three dimensions is the ability to understand and solve a problem with only a few of the total number of facts available. He then gave two examples of this type of problem. He continued by saying that Collier's syndrome was a slight but significant decrease in quantitative judgmental ability that resulted from underexposure to certain types of external stimulation in the adolescent formative years. He stressed that this underexposure could happen to anyone regardless of the quality of schooling they had experienced or their social and economic status. He then explained how the subject could have Collier's syndrome without having noticed any deficiency by saying that the discovery of Collier's syndrome was fairly recent and that the only noticeable effect connected with it was the tendency to make mistakes in problems requiring quantitative judgment— an effect that people typically attributed to momentary lapses of attention, lack of interest, or any number of other factors.

Following this discussion, the experimenter answered any questions that the subject had and then explained the nature of the diagnostic test the subject was to take. He said that each test problem required the subject to select one of four two-dimensional figures that matched a given three-dimensional figure. He indicated that shaded areas in the three-dimensional figure might be hidden from view in the two-dimensional figures. Thus, the test measured the subject's ability to solve problems without having all the relevant facts. He further indicated that the test problems would come in sets of three and that the subject would have about 45 seconds to work on each set. (In pretesting, the use of this type of test made it virtually impossible for the subject to determine how well he had done.) Following these instructions, the experimenter gave the subject two sample problems.

After the subject completed these problems, the camera/no-camera manipulation was introduced. In the camera conditions, the experimenter brought a TV camera mounted on a tripod over to the subject's table. He focused the camera on the subject, saying that the Institute sponsoring the study wanted a videotape of all participants. In the no-camera conditions, the TV camera remained in a corner of the experimental cubicle pointed toward the wall and was not mentioned by the experimenter.

Following the camera/no-camera manipulation, the experimenter gave the subject an IBM answer sheet, turned on the videotape of the diagnostic test, and left the room saying that he would return after the subject had completed the test. In 8 minutes, the experimenter returned, picked up the subject's answer sheet, and indicated that he would now take the test to the people in the computer room who would feed his answers into the computer. The computer would analyze his responses and determine whether he had Collier's syndrome and, if so, whether he had the potential to eliminate the deficiency. The experimenter then said that the director of the project needed to talk with him for a few minutes about tomorrow's schedule and that he might not be back before the computer analysis was finished. As he was leaving, he said that the subject could go ahead and look at the analysis if he wanted. Approximately 8 minutes after experimenter B left the cubicle, experimenter A gave a third, female experimenter (C) a folded computer printout, which constituted the can/cannot-reduce manipulation. Without looking at the contents of the printout, C entered the experimental cubicle and said she was from the computer room and had the completed analysis. She then placed the folded printout in front of the subject and said that the other experimenter would be back in a few minutes. In all cases, the subject, observed by experimenter A through a small opening, looked at the computer printout within 2 minutes after experimenter C left the room. In all conditions, the printout, which was fairly elaborate, indicated in bold type that the subject had Collier's syndrome. In the can-reduce conditions, the printout indicated that the subject had a 99.5% chance of totally eliminating the deficiency. In the cannot-reduce conditions, the printout indicated that the subject had a .5% chance of eliminating the deficiency.

In order to disassociate experimenter A's behavior from the Collier's syndrome study, A waited for about 10 minutes after experimenter C had given the printout to the subject; he then administered the set of questionnaires for a second time. After an additional 10 minutes, experimenter B reentered the cubicle and made sure that the subject had placed the questionnaires in the locked box. Picking up the printout, he casually asked the subject what the computer's analysis indicated. All subjects were able to report correctly what the printout said. Having verified that the subject had been exposed to the can/cannot-reduce manipulation, the experimenter discontinued the experiment and began debriefing. The experimenter was careful to make sure that the subject understood that there was no such thing as Collier's syndrome, that his responses to the test were not scored, and that the computer printout was bogus. To emphasize this last point, the experimenter showed the subject a printout that had results opposite to those given in his printout. During the course of debriefing, several subjects indicated that they had not believed the information on the printout. However, their data were included in the analysis and exclusion of these data in a second analysis did not appreciably change the results.

A scatterplot of the data indicated that the difference between the measures taken before and after the manipulation did not require a covariance analysis. Thus, an ANOVA was performed on the difference scores, and the results were clear. Subjects in the cannot-reduce conditions were more negative toward the experimenter and the experimental environment at time 2 than they were at time 1; in the can-reduce conditions, subjects' ratings of both the experimenter and the experimental environment tended to be slightly more positive at time 2 than at time 1 (Table 7.1). This difference was significant for ratings of the experimenter, $F(1, 45) = 12.87, p < .001$, and for ratings of the experimental situation, $F(1, 45) = 14.81, p < .001$. The presence of a significant camera/no-camera $\times$ can/cannot-reduce interaction, $F(1, 45) = 9.83, p < .01$, for attribution to experimenter, $F(1, 45) = 9.46, p < .01$, for attribution to the experimental situation, indicated that the presence of the camera accentuated these attributional tendencies as predicted. Conversely, levels of subjects' self-esteem in the can-

TABLE 7.1
Mean Changes in Evaluation Ratings of
Experimenter and Experimental Environment

Target of Rating		Can Reduce	Cannot Reduce
	No Camera	+ 1.31	− 10.46
Experimenter			
	Camera	+ .80	− 16.34
	No Camera	+ 1.93	− 7.63
Experiment			
	Camera	+ .53	− 10.21

Note: Means with positive signs represent changes toward positive evaluation; means with negative signs represent changes toward negative evaluation. As mean values increase, changes in evaluation become more positive (+) or negative (−).
  n = 14 for each condition.

TABLE 7.2
Mean Changes in Subjects'
Self-Esteem Ratings

	Can Reduce	Cannot Reduce
No Camera	− 14.44	+ 2.82
Camera	− 18.81	+ 4.32

Note: Means with positive signs represent changes toward higher self-esteem; means with negative signs represent changes toward lower self esteem. As mean values increase, self-esteem becomes higher (+) or lower (−).
  n = 14 for each condition.

not-reduce conditions showed a tendency to actually increase from time 1 to time 2, whereas subjects' self-esteem in the can-reduce conditions declined from time 1 to time 2, $F(1, 45) = 28.70$, $p <$ .001 (Table 7.2). The presence of a significant interaction between the possibility of reduction and the presence or absence of a camera, $F(1, 45) = 12.60$, $p < .01$, indicated that, as predicted, the presence of a camera accentuated the differences between can and cannot-reduce subjects' self-attributional tendencies.

The results of this experiment strongly suggest that belief in the possibility of eliminating a problem determines whether defensive attribution will occur. When subjects thought they could eliminate an intellectual deficiency by participating in a remedial program, their levels of self-esteem declined relative to pretest levels, but their evaluations of the experimenter and experimental situations did not change. We interpret this data pattern as reflecting attribution to self rather than a defensive attribution for the supposed deficiency. When the subjects thought that elimination of the problem was virtually impossible, their evaluation of the experimental situation and the experimenter became more negative, but their self-esteem showed a tendency to be more positive. We interpret this effect as indicating a defensive tendency to avoid locating the negative affect associated with the supposed intellectual deficiency in self by attributing that negative affect to something or someone external to self. In addition, the tendency for these subjects' levels of self-esteem to increase, though unexpected, certainly adds strength to the cost–benefit analysis of defensive attribution presented earlier. Not only does the person in the cannot-reduce conditions avoid lowered self-esteem through defensive attribution, but defensive attribution apparently increases self-esteem slightly (perhaps because the act of attributing responsibility for an intraself discrepancy externally involves reducing self-focus and increasing external focus—an event that objective self-awareness theory, Duval & Wicklund, 1972, predicts would elevate self-esteem). Thus, for the person who believes that coping with a self-related problem is all but impossible, the benefits, at least the psychodynamic benefits, of a defensive attribution clearly outweigh the immediate costs.

The relationship between self-focus, the ability to reduce an intraself discrepancy, and attributional tendency was in the predicted direction and entirely understandable. Increasing self-focus presumably increased the negativeness of the intraself discrepancy for subjects in both camera conditions. When coping was impossible, the increased negativeness enhanced the tendency to engage in defensive attribution. When subjects believed that the personal deficiency could be eliminated, increasing self-awareness produced the usual effect: increased attribution of the negative affect associated with the intraself discrepancy to self.

We are enthusiastic about the light that these results shed on the variables that determine whether the person will make a defensive attribution, but we should discuss the limitations of this study. First, the study did not measure causal attribution in terms of asking subjects to attribute causality for their deficiency to the standard categories of ability, effort, luck, and task difficulty primarily because these categories would probably have made little sense to subjects given the experimental situation. Therefore, the study did not provide a measure of causal attribution per se. However, we can make no sense out of the data without assuming that the subjects' causal attributions for the deficiency were being affected by the experimental manipulations in the predicted way. In addition, the important issues concerning defensive versus nondefensive attribution are not simply the locus of causality for a negative self-related event but also the consequences of that attribution. In our experiment, we see that defensive attribution leads to a negative evaluation of external stimuli, but self-attribution for the same problem lowers self-esteem.

Second, the dependent measures included questions about both the experimental environment and the experimenter. This procedure was used because we felt that subjects in the cannot-reduce conditions would attribute their experience of negative affect externally; however, we did not know which external stimulus would become the target of the attribution. As it turned out, subjects in the cannot-reduce conditions appear to have made a blanket attribution to all stimuli in their immediate external environment. This effect is unusual. The attribution process typically results in the identification of a particular stimulus as the cause of an effect rather than in an indiscriminate attribution. This characteristic of causal attribution suggests that the apparent dumping of causality in this experiment was due to the use of dependent measures that were too global in form and/or, for some reason, all stimuli connected with the experiment constituted a single possible cause for the subjects' experienced negative affect. Another alternative is that defensive-attribution processes do not result in a specific attribution to a particular and discrete external stimulus but yield something akin to an attributional halo effect. Regardless, the results of this experiment provide little information about the relative plausibility of these alternatives. The major purpose of conducting a second experiment was to test some ideas about what factors, if any, determine the target(s) of defensive attribution. Conducting a second study also provides an opportunity to replicate in part the findings in the Collier's syndrome study.

TARGETS OF DEFENSIVE
ATTRIBUTION

The theoretical basis for the first experiment included the assumption that people confronted with a problem go through a type of cost–benefit analysis at some level. For a person who cannot cope with a problem, defensive attribution coupled with the possibility of distancing oneself from the problem or conditions associated with the problem generates more benefits than costs. In the first experiment, subjects in the cannot-reduce conditions clearly avoided decreased self-esteem by attributing the negative affect associated with the supposed intellectual deficiency externally. We should keep in mind, however, that cannot-reduce subjects had negative affect to attribute at the time of the second measurement; otherwise, there would have been no affective basis for devaluing the experimenter and the experimental conditions. This fact suggests that defensive attribution (i.e., external attribution of negative affect) protects self-esteem but does not fully reduce, in and of itself, the negative affect generated at some level by the continued existence of the intraself discrepancy. This conclusion suggests that defensive attribution protects self-esteem when the person is proximate to stimuli associated with an intraself discrepancy but that full reduction of negative affect occurs only when the person is able to distance self from stimuli associated with the problem.

Let us extend this line of reasoning. Imagine a person who engaged in defensive attribution and successfully distanced himself/herself from stimuli associated with an intraself discrepancy. It follows that the person would experience an increase in negative affect shortly after encountering any stimulus that reminded him/her of the original difficulty. Furthermore, the temporal and spatial similarity between cognition of that reminder stimulus and the experience of increased negative affect should, according to the consistency principle, result in attribution for the increase in negative affect to that stimulus. In other words, any stimulus or set of conditions that reminds people of a problem they can do nothing about becomes the primary target for defensive attribution.

We find some merit in this reasoning. Specifically, this approach would explain why the cannot-reduce subjects in the Collier's syndrome study attributed negative affect to everything in the experimental setting. Almost everything in the experimental setting and particularly the experimenter was related to the supposed fact of the subject's deficiency if only through temporal and spatial proximity. Further, the overly general nature of the question concerning the experimental situation could have obscured any tendency for subjects to attribute more negative affect to those things that were more related to the deficiency such as the diagnostic test than to less-related aspects of the experimental setting such as the color of the walls in the cubicle.

In order to pursue this line of thought, an experiment (Duval, Mayer, Duval, & Depold, 1980) was designed that would allow some assessment of the validity of these ideas. Specifically, female subjects were led to believe that they were rated as either physically unattractive or attractive by a panel of beauty experts. They were then led to believe that they could (can-enhance conditions) or could not (cannot-enhance conditions) increase their physical attractiveness through cosmetic enhancement. After appropriate explanations, subjects were asked to rate the physical attractiveness of women who had been judged by pilot test subjects to be low, moderate, or high in physical attractiveness. They were also asked to rate these women in terms of the extent to which they possessed socially desirable or undesirable traits.

Because two stimuli that differ along some shared dimension are both scrutinized to a greater extent than noncontrasting stimuli (Berlyne, 1958), we expected the high attractive target to remind subjects in the unattractive cannot-enhance condition of their supposed deficit in physical attractiveness to a greater extent than would the moderate or low attractive target. In terms of our earlier reasoning, then, highly attractive women should become the targets of defensive attribution for subjects in the unattractive cannot-enhance condition and should be rated lower in physical attractiveness and degree of social desirability by those subjects than by subjects in any other condition. No between-condition differences in attractiveness and social desirability ratings should be found when the targets are moderate or low in physical attractiveness.

Participants in the study included 50 female undergraduates. Data from three subjects were excluded from the analysis due to overall suspicion of the cover story. These missing data were spread across three of the four conditions. The experimenter met individually with each subject. Subjects were randomly assigned to one of four conditions in a 2 (attractive/unattractive) × 2 (can-enhance/cannot-enhance) × 3 (low/moderate/high target attractiveness) factorial design with repeated measures on the third factor.

Each subject was seated at a table in front of a videotape camera and television monitor, which faced them throughout the experimental session. The experimenter explained that she had been employed by a major department store to assist in testing the effectiveness of a newly constructed computer program. This particular program was designed: (1) to analyze the critical features of each individual's overall facial structure; (2) to determine if that particular facial structure was amenable to cosmetic enhancement. The experimenter explained that the camera would scan the subject's facial features. The critical information regarding her appearance would be videotaped and relayed to an IBM computer. The computer program would then analyze her overall facial structure by synthesizing information regarding such major categories as skin tone, bone structure, lines, and symmetry of features. Subjects were told that the results of the analysis would be displayed on the television monitor before them and would conclude with an overall probability statement. This probability statement would indicate the extent to which the subject's facial structure was amenable to cosmetic enhancement.

At this point, the attractiveness manipulation was introduced. The experimenter told each subject that three cosmetological experts from the sponsoring department store were concealed behind the one-way mirror in the experimental cubicle. Further, the experimenter indicated that these experts had been judging the subject's personal level of physical attractiveness during the first part of the experimental session. This procedure was justified by explaining that the study required a normal distribution of attractiveness levels among participants in order to generalize the results of the study. The experimenter also indicated that in order to comply with prescribed experimental procedures the cosmetologists' ratings of the subject's physical attractiveness would be shown to the subject.

Following this explanation, the experimenter scanned each subject's facial features with the camera, explaining that it would require a few minutes for the analysis to be completed. She then left the room presumably to retrieve the attractiveness rating forms from the cosmetological experts. The experimenter returned, presented the attractiveness rating forms from each of the three judges to the subject, and told her that the ratings placed her in the upper (attractive condition) or lower (unattractive condition) 38% of physical attractiveness. In actuality, no cosmetologist rated the subject's attractiveness. The subject-attractiveness forms were prepared prior to each experimental session.

At this point, the experimenter explained that the analysis was completed and switched one of two previously videotaped computer printouts onto the television monitor. As the subject observed, the printout began with the headings: bone structure, musculature, and skin characteristics. The program ended with a probability statement regarding the amenability of the subject's facial structure to cosmetic enhancement. In the cannot-enhance conditions, the printout indicated that the probability the subject's facial structure was amenable to cosmetic enhancement was 2% of a possible 100%. In the can-enhance conditions, the printout indicated that the probability the subject's facial structure was amendable to cosmetic enhancement was 98% of a possible 100%. The experimenter briefly explained the meaning of the three preliminary facial analyses and concluded with the following statement: "The analysis indicates a 98% [2%] probability that your overall facial structure is amenable to cosmetic enhancement. That is a very high [low] probability that your facial structure is amenable to cosmetic enhancement." After the possibility of enhancement manipulation, each subject was informed that the first part of the study had been completed and that the second part was about to begin. The experimenter explained that this part of the experiment was designed to answer two questions: (1) are there regional or geographic preferences (or predispositions) toward specific physiognomic features? (2) is a person's physical appearance influenced by certain personality traits?

The subjects were requested to record their judgments of several stimulus persons (i.e., targets) in separate booklets. The targets were 5-by-7-inch color photographs of the faces of 10 college-aged women. A pilot study was conducted to determine which three target photographs were most representative of high, moderate, and low levels of attractiveness. The other seven photographs were used as filler items only. The booklets tapped impressions of each target along several dimensions. As in Dion, Berscheid, and Walster (1972) and Dermer and Thiel (1975), the first page of each booklet stressed the importance of rating each target person frankly. To emphasize the importance of this task further, subjects were told that the accuracy of a person's perception was the critical variable under study in the experiment.

The first item in each booklet requested the subjects to rate the facial attractiveness of all 10 target persons using a 10-point scale. This scale was anchored by the adjectives *attractive* and *unattractive*. Subjects were told to respond in terms of "how attractive you think each person is on the basis of the way you feel right now".

The second set of items (see Dion et al., 1972) requested subjects to rate each target person on 28 different personality traits. The 28 traits were randomly arranged and presented in a 6-point rating scale format. Fourteen of the 28 adjective traits constitute the Dion et al. (1972) Social Desirability Index. These 14 target adjective pairs were: *poised/awkward, modest/vain, strong/weak, interesting/boring, self-assertive/submissive, social/unsocial, independent/dependent, warm/cold, genuine/artificial, kind/cruel, exciting/dull, sexually warm/sexually cold, sincere/insincere,* and *sensitive/insensitive*. The other 14 adjective pairs were used as filler items only.

After the subjects completed rating each target person, they were individually and extensively debriefed. Special emphasis was given to the false nature of the feedback concerning their attractiveness ratings. Comments and questions were solicited from each subject concerning the plausibility of the cover story.

This study was designed to test one primary hypothesis: unattractive subjects who believe they cannot enhance their level of attractiveness should rate an attractive target lower in physical attractiveness and social desirability than should unattractive subjects who believe they can improve their appearance or subjects who believe they are themselves physically attractive. In order to test this hypothesis, a $2 \times 2 \times 3$ analysis of variance with repeated measures on the third factor was calculated for each of the two dependent measures.

The analysis of the perceived attractiveness data (Table 7.3) indicated a highly significant main effect for target attractiveness, F $(2, 86) = 217.38, p < .001$. However, the analysis also revealed the presence of a main effect for can/cannot-enhance, $F (1, 43) = 5.67, p < .02$. Given this effect, an analysis of the simple effects at each level of target attractiveness was conducted. The results of these analyses yielded the following conclusions. No significant interactions or main effects were found within the moderate or low target attractiveness conditions. However, the analysis did indicate a main effect for can/cannot-enhance within the high target attractiveness conditions, $F (1, 43) = 5.64, p < .04$. A planned comparison was calculated to define further the pattern of differences among the means within the high target attractiveness conditions. This analysis indicated that subjects in the cannot-enhance/ unattractive condition rated the high attractive target as significantly lower in physical attractiveness than did the average of the other three experimental conditions, $F (1, 43) = 4.34, p < .05$. Thus, although the effect of can/cannot-enhance on the ratings of target attractiveness initially appeared to be a main effect, internal analyses suggest that this effect was primarily due to the fact that, as predicted, subjects in the cannot-enhance/unattractive conditions rated high attractive targets lower in attractiveness than did subjects in the other three conditions.

The 14 items analogous to the Dion et al. Social Desirability Index were highly correlated and were combined for the purpose of analysis. The subjects' ratings of each of the three target persons

TABLE 7.3
Mean Perceived Attractiveness of Target Photo

	Subject Attractiveness					
	High			Low		
	Target Attractiveness			Target Attractiveness		
	High	Moderate	Low	High	Moderate	Low
Possibility of Cosmetic Enhancement						
Cannot	7.36	4.09	2.00	6.75	4.16	1.66
Can	8.00	5.00	2.18	7.61	4.46	1.92

Note: As means increase, perceived attractiveness of target increases.

TABLE 7.4
Mean Social Desirability Attributed to Targets

	Subject Attractiveness					
	High			Low		
	Target Attractiveness			Target Attractiveness		
	High	Moderate	Low	High	Moderate	Low
Possibility of Cosmetic Enhancement						
Cannot	67.19	62.09	49.73	60.00	61.08	49.08
Can	61.64	58.91	51.81	65.84	59.39	51.38

Note: As means increase, level of perceived social desirability increases.

(Table 7.4) on the 14 bipolar traits comprising this index were summed and averaged to determine the degree to which the subject attributed socially desirable traits to each. An analysis of variance was then performed on these data and revealed that subjects tended to attribute increasingly desirable social traits to targets as the level of target attractiveness increased, $F(2, 86) = 44.92, p < .001$. As discussed in Chapter 6, this effect is probably due to the tendency to match cause (the target) and the effects (the traits) on the dimension of affective sign and intensity. However, this main effect for target attractiveness was qualified by the presence of a marginal target × possibility of enhancement × attractiveness interaction, $F(2, 86) = 2.64$, $p < .08$.

Given the tendency toward an interaction, analyses of the simple effects at each level of target attractiveness were performed. The analysis of the simple effects in the high target attractiveness conditions indicated a significant possibility of enhancement × attractiveness interaction, $F(1, 43) = 6.03$, $p < .03$. Similar analyses conducted for the moderate and low levels of target attractiveness yielded nonsignificant results for all main effects and interactions, $F < 1$. To define further the pattern of the possibility of enhancement × attractiveness interaction in the high target attractiveness conditions, a planned comparison was carried out. This analysis indicated that subjects in the cannot-enhance/unattractive condition rated the high attractive target as lower in social desirability than did subjects in the other three conditions, although this effect attained only a marginal level of significance, $F(1, 43) = 3.39$, $p < .07$. Thus, the results of the simple effects and planned comparison tests suggest that the target attractiveness × possibility of enhancement × subject attractiveness interaction was primarily due to the fact that, as predicted, subjects in the cannot-enhance/unattractive condition rated high attractive targets lower in social desirability than subjects in the other three conditions.

Taken together, results from the two studies discussed in this chapter identify the variable of being able versus not being able to cope with a problem as the (or a) primary determinant of defensive as opposed to nondefensive attribution. When subjects in the first experiment believed they could reduce or eliminate an intraself problem, self-attribution of causality for the negative affect generated by that problem occurred. When subjects believed the intraself problem to be virtually unsolvable, they protected self-esteem by attributing the negative affect generated by the problem externally. In addition, the second experiment indicates that this attribution is not indiscriminant. The target or targets of defensive attribution will be those stimuli that remind the person of or, more generally stated, are associated with the problem. This mechanism will probably prove critical for a causal attribution-mediated model of behavior. It should also be useful in the attempt to make sense of the labyrinth that research on self-attribution for success and failure now constitutes.

Before concluding this chapter, we should comment more fully on the relationship between the defensive attribution mechanism and our general approach to causal attribution. As indicated in the introduction, we do not find theories of attribution based on assumptions of general tendencies to distort cause and effect relationships in order to maintain illusions of high self-esteem, control over the world, etc., acceptable. Yet in this chapter we seem to embrace a concept that shares common ground with those approaches: the notion that people will protect self-esteem. This is, to some extent, the case. However, the other side of the coin is that we have cut the influence of this motive on attribution in half, so to speak, by showing that defensive attributional tendencies are evident only if the person believes that he or she cannot cope with the problem. When coping is believed possible, no defensiveness is apparent in attribution, and we assume that attributional processes are again governed by the consistency principle. Furthermore, even though we found a tendency for enhanced self-esteem to covary with defensive attribution, a more parsimonious explanation for this effect involves decreased self-focus rather than a motive to consistently attribute all good things to self and bad things to external factors.

Thus, although we are not prepared at this time to debunk totally the notion that some ego function distorts reality in service of its own selfish needs, we feel that progress in that direction has been made.

Epilogue

In essence we have presented a theory of causal attribution based on one major premise. To maximize simplicity, consciousness connects cognized effects with cognized possible causes such that consistency between the elements of cause–effect unit formations is maximal. We have defined consistency in terms of similarity between the properties of cognized effects and possible causes and applied the formulation to the dimensions of time, space, focalization, and affect. In doing so, we have been able to account for most of the major phenomena that have received attention from researchers in the area of causal attribution as well as laying the groundwork for an attributional approach to phenomena previously considered to be nonattributional in nature. Thus, we conclude that the goal-directed model provides a more integrated and viable approach to the diversity of attribution phenomena than do nongoal-directed models. This does not mean that we consider the present theory to be complete. For example, we do not know how degrees of similarity on the four dimensions (i.e., time, space, focalization, and affect) combine to determine the overall degree of similarity between cognized events. Hopefully the function will be additive. However, even if additive, we do not know whether similarity on the various dimensions is weighted equally or whether one dimension (e.g., time) is more influential in determining similarity between cognized events than are other dimensions. In addition, it would probably be foolish to assume that time, space, focalization, and affect constitute the total set of properties that influence causal attribution. However, in spite of these unanswered questions, we believe that the basic principles we have set forth will stand the test of time. Proof or disproof of this conclusion will of course take time, creativity, and the critical talents of those involved in cognitive psychology.

References

Adams, D. L. Correlates of satisfaction among the elderly. *Gerontologist*, 1971, *11*, 64-68.

Amster, H. Evaluative judgment and recall in incidental learning. *Journal of Verbal Learning and Verbal Behavior*, 1964, *3*, 446-473.

Anderson, N. H. Averaging versus adding as a stimulus combination rule in impression formation. *Journal of Experimental Psychology*, 1965, *70*, 394-400.

Anisfeld, M., & Lambert, W. E. When are pleasant words learned faster than unpleasant words? *Journal of Verbal Learning and Verbal Behavior*, 1966, *5*, 132-141.

Arkin, R. M., & Duval, S. Focus of attention and causal attribution of actors and observers. *Journal of Experimental Social Psychology*, 1975, *11*, 427-438.

Aronson, E., & Mills, J. The effect of severity of initiation on liking for a group. *Journal of Abnormal and Social Psychology*, 1959, *59*, 177-181.

August, G. J., Rychlak, J. F., & Felker, D. W. Affective assessment, self-concept, and the verbal learning styles of 5th grade children. *Journal of Educational Psychology*, 1975, *67*, 801-806.

Averill, J. R. A semantic atlas of emotional concepts. JSAS *Catalog of Selected Documents in Psychology*, 1975, *5*, 330. (Ms. No. 421)

Bahrick, H. P., Fitts, P. M., & Rankin, R. E. Effect of incentives upon reactions to peripheral stimuli. *Journal of Experimental Psychology*, 1952, *44*, 400-406.

Bandura, A. *Principles of behavior modification*. New York: Holt, Rinehart & Winston, 1969.

Bem, D. J. An experimental analysis of self-persuasion. *Journal of Experimental Social Psychology*, 1965, *1*, 199-218.

Berkowitz, L. The contagion of violence: An S-R mediational analysis of some effects of observed aggression. In M. Page (Ed.), *Nebraska Symposium on Motivation* (Vol. 19). Lincoln, Neb. University of Nebraska Press, 1971.

Berkowitz, L. Some determinants of impulsive aggression: Role of mediated associations with reinforcements for aggression. *Psychological Review*, 1974, *81*, 165–176.

Berkowitz, L., & Knurek, D. A. Label-mediated hostility generalization. *Journal of Personality and Social Psychology*, 1969, *13*, 200–206.

Berlyne, D.E. The influence of complexity and novelty in visual figures on orienting responses. *Journal of Experimental Psychology*, 1958, *55*, 287–296.

Berlyne, D. E. Attention as a problem in behavior theory. In D. I. Mostofsky (Ed.), *Attention: Contemporary theory and analysis*. New York: Appleton-Century-Crofts, 1970.

Bradley, G. W. Self-serving biases in the attribution process: A reexamination of the fact or fiction question. *Journal of Personality and Social Psychology*, 1978, *36*, 56-71.

Brenner, M. The next-in-line effect. *Journal of Verbal Learning and Verbal Behavior*, 1973, *12*, 320–323.

Bresnahan, J. L., & Shapiro, M. M. A general equation and technique for the exact partitioning of chi-square contingency tables. *Psychological Bulletin*, 1966, *66*, 252–262.

Bruning, J. L., Capage, J. W., Kozoh, G. F., Young, P.F., & Young, W. E. Socially induced drive and range of cue utilization. *Journal of Personality and Social Psychology*, 1968, *9*, 242–244.

Bursill, A. E. The restriction of peripheral vision during exposure to hot and humid conditions. *Quarterly Journal of Experimental Psychology*, 1958, *10*, 113–129.

Bush, L. E., II. Successive-intervals scaling of adjectives denoting feelings. JSAS *Catalog of Selected Documents in Psychology*, 1972, *2*, 140. (Ms. No. 262).

Craik, F. I. M., & Lockhart, R. S. Levels of processing: A framework for memory research. *Journal of Verbal Learning and Verbal Behavior*, 1972, *11*, 671–684.

Davison, G. C. Systematic desensitization as a counter-conditioning process. *Journal of Abnormal Psychology*, 1968, *73*, 91–99.

Dawes, R. M., Singer, D., & Lemons, F. An experimental analysis of the contrast effect and its implications for inter-group communication and the indirect assessment of attitude. *Journal of Personality and Social Psychology*, 1972, *21*, 281–295.

Dermer, M., & Thiel, D. L. When beauty may fail. *Journal of Personality and Social Psychology*, 1975, *31*, 1168–1176.

Dion, K., Berscheid, E., & Walster, E. What is beautiful is good. *Journal of Personality and Social Psychology*, 1972, *24*, 285–290.

Dollard, J., Doob, L. W., Miller, N. E., Mowrer, O. H., & Sears, R. R. *Frustration and aggression*. New Haven, Conn.: Yale University Press, 1939.

Duval, S.   Conformity on a visual task as a function of personal novelty on attitudinal dimensions and being reminded of the object status of self. *Journal of Experimental Social Psychology*, 1976, *12*, 87–98.

Duval, S., & Duval, V. H.   *Novelty and causal attribution.* Paper presented at the meeting of the Western Psychological Association, Seattle, Wash., 1977.

Duval, S., & Duval, V. H.   *Salience or similarity: A test of the relationship between focus of attention and causal attribution.* Unpublished manuscript, University of Southern California, 1979.

Duval, S., Duval, V. H., & Neely, R.   Self-focus, felt responsibility, and helping behavior. *Journal of Personality and Social Psychology*, 1979, *37*, 1769–1778.

Duval, S., & Hensley, V.   Extensions of objective self-awareness theory: The focus of attention-causal attribution hypothesis. In J. H. Harvey, W. J. Ickes, & R. F. Kidd (Eds.), *New directions in attribution research* (Vol. 1). Hillsdale, N.J.: Lawrence Erlbaum Associates, 1976.

Duval, S., Jellison, J. M., & Woodward, C.   *Success, self-esteem, objective self-awareness and time.* Paper presented at the meeting of the American Psychological Association, Toronto, 1978.

Duval, S., Mayer, F. S., Duval, V. H., & Depold, C.   *Targets of defensive attribution.* Unpublished manuscript, University of Southern California, 1980.

Duval, S., & Siegel, K. N.   *Some determinants of objective self-awareness: Quantitative novelty.* Paper presented at the meeting of the American Psychological Association, Toronto, 1978.

Duval, S., & Wicklund, R. A.   *A theory of objective self-awareness.* New York: Academic Press, 1972.

Duval, S., & Wicklund, R. A.   Effects of objective self-awareness on attribution of causality. *Journal of Experimental Social Psychology*, 1973, *9*, 17–31.

Easterbrook, J.A.   The effect of emotion on cue utilization and the organization of behavior. *Psychological Review*, 1959, *66*, 183–201.

Feather, N. T., & Simon, J. G.   Attribution of responsibility and valence of outcome in relation to initial confidence and success and failure of self and other. *Journal of Personality and Social Psychology*, 1971, *18*, 173–188.

Federoff, N. A., & Harvey, J. H.   Focus of attention, self-esteem and attribution of causality. *Journal of Research in Personality*, 1976, *10*, 336–345.

Festinger, L.   *A theory of cognitive dissonance.* Evanston, Ill.: Row, Peterson, 1957.

Firestone, I. J., Kaplan, K. J., & Russell, J. C.   Anxiety, fear, and affiliation with similar-state versus dissimilar-state others: Misery sometimes loves non-miserable company. *Journal of Personality and Social Psychology*, 1973, *26*, 409–414.

Fishbein, M.   Attitude and the prediction of behavior. In M. Fishbein (Ed.), *Readings in attitude theory and measurement.* New York: Wiley, 1967.

Freedman, J. L.   Role playing: Psychology by consensus. *Journal of Personality and Social Psychology*, 1969, *13*, 107–114.

Frieze, I. H.   Causal attributions and information seeking to explain success and failure. *Journal of Research in Personality*, 1976, *10*, 293–305.

Frieze, I. H., & Weiner, B.   Cue utilization and attributional judgments for success and failure. *Journal of Personality*, 1971, *39*, 591–606.

Geller, D. M.   Involvement in role-playing simulations: A demonstration with studies on obedience. *Journal of Personality and Social Psychology*, 1978, *36*, 219–235.

Geller, V., & Shaver, P.   Cognitive consequences of self-awareness. *Journal of Experimental Social Psychology*, 1976, *12*, 99–108.

Gerard, H. B., & Mathewson, G. C.   The effects of severity of initiation on liking for a group: A replication. *Journal of Experimental Social Psychology*, 1966, *2*, 278–287.

Girodo, M.   Film-induced arousal, information search, and the attribution process. *Journal of Personality and Social Psychology*, 1973, *25*, 357–360.

Glass, D. C., & Singer, J. E.   *Urban stress: Experiments on noise and social stressors.* New York: Academic Press, 1972.

Gregory, R. L.   *Eye and brain: The psychology of seeing.* New York: McGraw-Hill, 1970.

Grings, W. W.   The role of consciousness and cognition in autonomic behavior change. In F. J. McGuigan & R. A. Schoonover (Eds.), *The psychophysiology of thinking: Studies of covert processes.* New York: Academic Press, 1973.

Grings, W. W., Givens, M. C., & Carey, C. A.   Contingency contrast effects in discrimination conditioning. *Journal of Experimental Psychology: General*, 1979, *108*, 281–295.

Hansen, R. D., & Donoghue, J. M.   The power of consensus: Information derived from one's own and others' behavior. *Journal of Personality and Social Psychology*, 1977, *35*, 294–302.

Harvey, J. H., Arkin, R. M., Gleason, J. M., & Johnston, S.   Effect of expected and observed outcome of an action on the differential causal attributions of actor and observer. *Journal of Personality*, 1974, *42*, 62–77.

Heider, F.   Social perception and phenomenal causality. *Psychological Review*, 1944, *51*, 358–374.

Heider, F.   *The psychology of interpersonal relations.* New York: Wiley, 1958.

Holmes, D. S.   Differential change in affective intensity and the forgetting of unpleasant personal experiences. *Journal of Personality and Social Psychology*, 1970, *15*, 234–239.

Holmes, D. S., & Bennett, D. H.   Experiments to answer questions raised by the use of deception in psychological research. *Journal of Personality and Social Psychology*, 1974, *29*, 358–367.

Insko, C. A., Songer, E., & McGarvey, W.   Balance, positivity, and agreement in the Jordan Paradigm: A defense of balance theory. *Journal of Experimental Social Psychology*, 1974, *10*, 53–83.

Isen, A. M., Shalker, T. E., Clark, M., & Karp, L.   Affect, accessibility of material in memory, and behavior: A cognitive loop? *Journal of Personality and Social Psychology*, 1978, *36*, 1–12.

Jones, E. E., & Davis, K. E.   From acts to dispositions: The attribution process in person perception. In L. Berkowitz (Ed.), *Advances in experimental social psychology* (Vol. 2). New York: Academic Press, 1965.

Jones, E. E., Davis, K. E., & Gergen, K. J.   Role playing variations and their informational value for person perception. *Journal of Abnormal and Social Psychology*, 1961, *63*, 302–310.

Jones, E. E., & Harris, V. A.   The attribution of attitudes. *Journal of Experimental Social Psychology*, 1967, *3*, 1–24.

Jones, E. E., & Nisbett, R. E.   The actor and the observer: Divergent perceptions of the causes of behavior. In E. E. Jones, D. E. Kanouse, H. H. Kelley, R. E. Nisbett, S. Valins & B. Weiner (Eds.), *Attribution: Perceiving the causes of behavior*. Morristown, N.J.: General Learning Press, 1971.

Jones, S. C.   Self- and interpersonal evaluations: Esteem theories versus consistency theories. *Psychological Bulletin*, 1973, *79*, 185–199.

Kahneman, D.   *Attention and effort*. Englewood Cliffs, N.J.: Prentice Hall, 1973.

Kassin, S. M.   Consensus information, prediction, and causal attribution: A review of the literature and issues. *Journal of Personality and Social Psychology*, 1979, *37*, 1966–1981.

Kelley, H. H.   Attribution theory in social psychology. In D. Levine (Ed.), *Nebraska Symposium on Motivation* (Vol. 15). Lincoln: University of Nebraska Press, 1967.

Kelley, H. H.   Attribution in social interaction. In E. E. Jones, D. E. Kanouse, H. H. Kelley, R. E. Nisbett, S. Valins & B. Weiner (Eds.), *Attribution: Perceiving the causes of behavior*. Morristown, N.J.: General Learning Press, 1971.

Kelley, H. H.   The processes of causal attribution. *American Psychologist*, 1973, *28*, 107–128.

Keppel, G.   Word value and verbal learning. *Journal of Verbal Learning and Verbal Behavior*, 1963, *1*, 353–356.

Koffka, K.   *Principles of gestalt psychology*. New York: Harcourt, Brace, 1935.

Konecni, V. J., & Sargent-Pollock, D.   Choice between melodies differing in complexity under divided-attention conditions. *Journal of Experimental Psychology: Human Perception and Performance*, 1976, *2*, 347–356.

Kruglanski, A. W.   The human subject in the psychological experiment: Fact and artifact. In L. Berkowitz (Ed.), *Advances in experimental social psychology* (Vol. 8). New York: Academic Press, 1975.

Kulik, J. A., & Taylor, S. E.   Premature consensus on consensus? Effects of sample-based versus self-based consensus information. *Journal of Personality and Social Psychology*, 1980, *38*, 871–878.

Langer, E. J., & Imber, L.   Role of mindlessness in the perception of deviance. *Journal of Personality and Social Psychology*, 1980, *39*, 360–367.

Lynn, R.   *Attention, arousal, and the orientation response*. Elmsford, N.Y.: Pergamon Press, 1966.

McArthur, L. A.   The how and what of why: Some determinants and consequences of causal attribution. *Journal of Personality and Social Psychology*, 1972, *22*, 171–193.

McArthur, L. Z., & Post, D. L.   Figural emphasis and person perception. *Journal of Experimental Social Psychology*, 1977, *13*, 520–535.

McArthur, L. Z., & Solomon, L. K.   Perceptions of an aggressive encounter as a function of the victim's salience and the perceiver's arousal. *Journal of Personality and Social Psychology*, 1978, *36*, 1278–1290.

Mehrabian, A., & Russell, J. A.   *An approach to environmental psychology.* Cambridge, Mass.: MIT Press, 1974.

Michotte, A. E.   The emotions regarded as functional connections. In M. L. Reymert (Ed.), *Feelings and emotions.* New York: Hafner, 1950.

Michotte, A. E.   *The perception of causality.* New York: Basic Books, 1963.

Miller, A. G.   Role of physical attractiveness in impression formation. *Psychonomic Science*, 1970, *19*, 241–243.

Miller, D. T., & Ross, M.   Self-serving biases in the attribution of causality: Fact or fiction? *Psychological Bulletin*, 1975, *82*, 213–225.

Nisbett, R. E., & Borgida, E.   Attribution and the psychology of prediction. *Journal of Personality and Social Psychology*, 1975, *32*, 932–943.

Nisbett, R. E., Caputo, C., Legant, P., & Marecek, J.   Behavior as seen by the actor and as seen by the observer. *Journal of Personality and Social Psychology*, 1973, *27*, 154–164.

Nisbett, R. E., & Schachter, S.   Cognitive manipulation of pain. *Journal of Experimental Social Psychology*, 1966, *2*, 227–236.

Nisbett, R. E., & Wilson, T. D.   Telling more than we can know: Verbal reports on mental processes. *Psychological Review*, 1977, *84*, 231–259.

Norman, D. A.   *Memory and attention: An introduction to human information processing.* (2nd ed.), New York: Wiley, 1976.

Osgood, C. E.   Studies on the generality of affective meaning systems.   *American Psychologist*, 1962, *17*, 10–28.

Osgood, C. E.   Semantic differential technique in the comparative study of cultures. *American Anthropologist*, 1964, *66*, 171–200.

Osgood, C. E.   On the whys and wherefores of E, P, and A. *Journal of Personality and Social Psychology*, 1969, *12*, 194–199.

Osgood, C. E., May, W. H., & Miron, M. S.   *Cross-cultural universals of affective meaning.* Urbana: University of Illinois Press, 1975.

Osgood, C. E., Suci, G. J., & Tannenbaum, P. H.   *The measurement of meaning.* Urbana: University of Illinois Press, 1957.

Pryor, J. B., & Kriss, M.   The cognitive dynamics of salience in the attribution process. *Journal of Personality and Social Psychology*, 1977, *35*, 49–55.

Regan, D. T., Straus, E., & Fazio, R.   Liking and the attribution process. *Journal of Experimental Social Psychology*, 1974, *10*, 385–397.

Regan, D. T. & Totten, J.   Empathy and attribution: Turning observers into actors. *Journal of Personality and Social Psychology*, 1975, *32*, 850–856.

Rogers, C.   Therapy, personality and interpersonal relationships. In S. Koch (Ed.), *Psychology: A study of a science* (Vol. 3). New York: McGraw-Hill, 1959.

Ross, L.   The intuitive psychologist and his shortcomings: Distortions in the attribution process. In L. Berkowitz (Ed.), *Advances in experimental social psychology*, (Vol. 10). New York: Academic Press, 1977.

Ross, L., Greene, D., & House, P.   The "false consensus effect": An egocentric bias in social perception and attribution processes. *Journal of Experimental Social Psychology*, 1977, *13*, 279–301.

Ross, L., Rodin, J., & Zimbardo, P. G.   Toward an attribution therapy: The reduction of fear through induced cognitive-emotional misattribution. *Journal of Personality and Social Psychology*, 1969, *12*, 279–288.

Rudner, R. S.   *Philosophy of social science*. Englewood Cliffs, N.J.: Prentice-Hall, 1966.

Russell, J. A.   Evidence of convergent validity on the dimensions of affect. *Journal of Personality and Social Psychology*, 1978, *36*, 1152–1168.

Rychlak, J. F., Carlsen, N. L., & Dunning, L. P.   Personal adjustment and the free recall of materials with affectively positive or negative meaningfulness. *Journal of Abnormal Psychology*, 1974, *83*, 480–487.

Schachter, S.   The interaction of cognitive and physiological determinants of emotional state. In L. Berkowitz (Ed.), *Advances in experimental social psychology*. (Vol. 1). New York: Academic Press, 1964.

Scheier, M. F., & Carver, C. S.   Self-focused attention and the experience of emotion: Attraction, repulsion, elation and depression. *Journal of Personality and Social Psychology*, 1977, *35*, 624–636.

Singerman, K. J., Borkovec, T. D., & Baron, R. S.   Failure of a "misattribution therapy" manipulation with a clinically relevant target behavior. *Behavior Therapy*, 1976, *7*, 306–313.

Spence, J. T., & Spence, K. W.   The motivational components of manifest anxiety: Drive and drive stimuli. In C. D. Spielberger (Ed.), *Anxiety and behavior*. New York: Academic Press, 1966.

Storms, M. D.   Videotape and the attribution process: Reversing actors' and observers' point of view. *Journal of Personality and Social Psychology*, 1973, *27*, 165–175.

Taylor, S. E., Crocker, J., Fiske, S. T., Sprinzen, M., & Winkler, J. D.   The generalizability of salience effects. *Journal of Personality and Social Psychology*, 1979, *37*, 357–368.

Taylor, S. E., & Fiske, S. T.   Point of view and perceptions of causality. *Journal of Personality and Social Psychology*, 1975, *32*, 439–445.

Taylor, S. E., & Fiske, S. T.   Salience, attention and attribution: Top of the head phenomenon. In L. Berkowitz (Ed.), *Advances in experimental social psychology*. (Vol. 11). New York: Academic Press, 1978.

Testa, T. J.   Effects of similarity of location and temporal intensity pattern of conditioned and unconditioned stimuli on the acquisition of conditioned suppression in rats. *Journal of Experimental Psychology: Animal Behavior Processes*, 1975, *104*, 114–121.

Tesser, A., & Conlee, M. C.   Some effects of time and thought on attitude polarization, *Journal of Personality and Social Psychology*, 1975, *31*, 262–270.

Thurstone, L. L.   Theory of attitude measurement. *Psychological Bulletin*, 1929, *36*, 222–241.

Trimble, R. R., & Brink, T. D. T.   Incidental learning of CVC trigrams as a function of polarization and affectivity. *Psychological Reports*, 1969, *25*, 586.

Tversky, A.   Features of similarity. *Psychological Review*, 1977, *84*, 327–352.

Tversky, A., & Kahneman, D.   Availability: A heuristic for judging frequency and probability. *Cognitive Psychology*, 1973, *5*, 207–232.

Upshaw, H. S.   The personal reference scale: An approach to social judgment. In L. Berkowitz (Ed.) *Advances in experimental social psychology*. New York: Academic Press, 1968.

Velten, E. C., Jr.   *The induction of elation and depression through the reading of structured sets of mood-statements.* Unpublished doctoral dissertation, University of Southern California, 1967.

Wells, G. L., & Harvey, J. H.   Do people use consensus information in making causal attributions? *Journal of Personality and Social Psychology*, 1977, *35*, 279–293.

Wicklund, R. A., Cooper, J., & Linder, E. L.   Effects of expected effort on attitude change prior to exposure. *Journal of Experimental Social Psychology*, 1967, *3*, 416–428.

Willis, R. H., & Willis, Y. A.   Role playing versus deception: An experimental comparison. *Journal of Personality and Social Psychology*, 1970, *16*, 472–477.

Wine, J.   Test anxiety and direction of attention. *Psychological Bulletin*, 1971, *76*, 92–104.

Young, P. T.   The role of affective processes in learning and motivation. *Psychological Review*, 1959, *66*, 104–125.

Zanna, M. P., Kiesler, C. A., & Pilkonis, P. A.   Positive and negative attitudinal affect established by classical conditioning. *Journal of Personality and Social Psychology*, 1970, *14*, 321–328.

Author Index

Numbers in *italics* denote pages with bibliographic information.

Subject Index

A

Affect, 85-111
  and attribution, 89-111
  and cognition, 86
  conditioning of, 95-96
  and memory, 88-89
  nature of, 85
  and perception, 87-88, 103-104
Asymmetry criteria, 7-11
  and magnitude, 10-11
  and time, 9-10
Attitudes, 111

B

Balance model, 106-108
"Beautiful is good" stereotype,
  reinterpretation of, 109

C

Cause-effect unit formation, 1-2, 7-8
  asymmetrical nature of, 7-8
  description of, 1-2
Cognitive processes, 87-89, 103-104
  memory, 88-89
  perception, 87-88, 103-104
Cognitive processing, models of, i-ii, 1-4,
  106-108

C

Consensus information, 67-68, 72-74
Consistency principle, 3-7, 17-20, 40-45,
  91-93
  definition of, 5-7
  operation of, 3-5, 17-20, 40-50, 91-93
Coping ability and defensive attribution,
  117-124
Correspondent inference theory, 66-67
Covariation, 21-23, 32

D

Defensive attribution, 114-133
  cost/benefit analysis of, 114-115
  targets of, 126-133
Distinctiveness information, 68
Dynamism, 48-49
  definition of, 48
  and focus of attention, 48-49

E

Effect event, definition of, 1-2
Effort-justification effect, attributional
  analysis of, 24-32

F

Figure-ground, 37, 39
Focal consciousness, operation of, 35-39